Praise for *Work for What's Next*

"*Work for What's Next* challenges the toxic norms we've come to accept about work—from bad bosses and grueling schedules to soul-crushing commutes. Amanda Schneider maps a new vision grounded in flexibility, trust, and collective purpose. Backed by solid research, the book offers a roadmap for making work work better—for leaders seeking enduring success, managers empowering teams without burnout, and employees looking for an alternative to the false trade-off between having a life and earning a living."

—Kate Lister,
President, Global Workplace Analytics

"The friction we're experiencing at work isn't generational—it's structural. Amanda Schneider brings rare clarity to what's breaking beneath the surface and offers leaders a practical guide for navigating what comes next with humility, transparency, and purpose."

—Rex Miller,
Futurist and bestselling author

"Relevant and thought-provoking. I find myself referencing themes from this book in leadership conversations because it is all so relevant to the conversations we are having internally. I can't wait to put a copy in the hands of every manager on my team."

—Natalie Hartkopf,
CEO, Hightower

"*Work for What's Next* is a sharp, urgent call to rethink how we work - powered by the generation ready to rebuild it. Amanda helps us navigate these often-murky waters with honest dialogue, research, and insight. A must read!"

—Brett Shwery,
Global Interior Design Director, HKS

"No one has a better 360° view of modern work than Amanda Schneider. Sharp, research-packed, and unapologetically practical, she translates generational insight into real-world shifts that help leaders rethink the rules and redesign how work actually gets done."

—**Brant Menswar,**
CEO of Black Sheep Foundry and bestselling author

"Incredibly insightful and actionable. The future is bright for leaders who choose to embrace the changes shaping our teams, clients, and communities. Grounded in trust, Amanda shows how intentional 'phygital' spaces can drive stronger connection, communication, and collaboration."

—**Jason McCann,**
CEO, Vari

"Amanda brings the rare combination of experience and intellectual curiosity needed to challenge the status quo. She pairs a clear-eyed view of today's workplace challenges with practical solutions and a compelling vision for what comes next. What once felt like a cyclical generational divide now feels solvable—by intentionally involving every generation in the solution. I look forward to applying these insights through this powerful lens."

—**Olivia Danielson,**
Senior Project Interior Designer, HOK

"Amanda has a rare ability to pair hard data with human narrative, exposing the generational friction quietly eroding workplaces. More than a diagnosis, she delivers concrete solutions that help multiple generations find their rhythm together. *Work for What's Next* might just save the future of work—and your sanity."

—**Kendra Johnson,**
Founder of The Venned Group and
Canada's leading soft skills expert

"Part manifesto, part playbook, this book is a bold call to redesign how we work—and the environments that support it. It's a vision not just for tomorrow's workforce, but for everyone."

—**Bethany Parks,**
Director of Sales, Source Seating

"*Work for What's Next* brings together stories, data, and thoughtful analysis to capture what we're collectively experiencing in today's workforce—and offers a clear framework for how individuals and organizations can move forward with intention."

—**Corianne Burrell,**
Senior Project Manager, Perkins&Will

"This isn't a generational manual—it's a data-driven, story-centered guide to honest dialogue and real change. Each chapter reframes familiar concepts with fresh insight, breaking stereotypes and turning them into practical tools leaders can act on. For organizations navigating an evolving workforce, this book is a gold mine—an invitation to humanize the workplace, build empathetic leadership, and create cultures people want to be part of."

—**Megan DeTratto,**
Co-Founder, TOKONEXT Talent Solutions

"*Work for What's Next* gives voice to what both emerging professionals and senior leaders have been feeling about the modern workplace. With clarity and conviction, Amanda turns uncertainty into insight—revealing how our culture is evolving and what it means for each of us. By illuminating the strengths of Gen Z and the generations rising behind them, this book replaces confusion with possibility. Inspiring and deeply resonant, it empowers readers to lead, collaborate, and thrive in a future we can shape—together."

—**Chelsea Beardsley,**
Interior Designer, Clark & Enersen

"Amanda Schneider is widely regarded as a leading authority on workplace strategy. Grounded in rigorous research and thoughtful interviews, her insights are not only timely but transformative. Her commitment to uncovering what's next makes her an invaluable voice for anyone seeking to understand the future of work."

—**Marilyn McSweeny,**
Principal, The McSweeny Group Executive Recruiting

FOREWORD BY
DEBORAH GOLDEN, Deloitte Innovation Leader + TEDx Speaker

Amanda Schneider

Work
for What's
Next

Why Workplace Culture is Failing and How the Next Generation Can Fix It

WILEY

For my mom and dad who taught me girls could do anything boys could do. For my elephant circle of women who made that possible.

And for my sons, who remind me daily that the next generation will do even more.

Contents

Foreword

—By Deborah Golden

THERE IS A DISTINCT tension vibrating through the modern organization. It is the sound of a 21st-century technological capability griding against a 20th-century management philosophy. While digital infrastructures have shifted to the cloud, many operating systems remain anchored in earlier eras, creating a drag coefficient that can stall even our boldest attempts at progress.

We find ourselves in a paradoxical state: possessing the tools of ubiquity, the ability to work from anywhere at any time, yet remaining bound by "systems" that often equate presence with performance. However, this disconnect is not merely a matter of geography; it can fundamentally fracture strategic intent as well. Organizations often champion innovation in mission statements, yet tend to gravitate to the conformity of familiar routines that can inadvertently slow the very future we are trying to build—today.

It is time to admit a hard truth: the mechanism of work as we know it has flaws.

But in this breaking there is a vast opening. An opportunity.

Across three decades of leading transformation and innovation, I have found that the greatest barrier to progress is rarely a lack of new ideas, but the persistence of old ones. We operate systems wired for preservation, creating a friction that can diminish our innate drive to innovate. This tension contributes to the disconnect felt in our workplaces today—the "trust gap," the burnout, and the quiet disengagement. To navigate this gap, we need to learn differently while also simultaneously unlearning what we *think* we know.

Unlearning is not a passive act of erasure; it is a metabolic process of breaking down the very structures that once made us feel secure. It is a courageous act of leadership, requiring the antifragility to stand in the fire of uncertainty and trust that something stronger will emerge on the other side. Crucially, this situation does not mean that experience is obsolete, quite the contrary. In an age of infinite information, our most critical asset is wisdom: the hard-won ability to discern signals from the noise. True transformation doesn't happen when we replace the past, it happens when we combine our collective wisdom to pressure-test the future.

As artificial intelligence commoditizes "knowing" by delivering answers in milliseconds, the very definition of value shifts; it no longer lies in the answer, but in the architecture of the inquiry. It evolves in the willingness to unlearn our reliance on the easy path and relearn through the curiosity of transformation.

I know this because I have lived it. There have been moments in my own life—navigating the high-stakes environments of leadership and life—where I expanded my definition of resilience; reframing that a "perfect" career or life is not always a straight line, but a dynamic evolution that can provide the greatest opportunity for growth. Sometimes, unlearning means acknowledging that the systems we spent a lifetime navigating were not fully designed for the future we now face and finding the courage to build new ones in real time.

Work for What's Next is a field guide for this act of unlearning. Through the lens of ThinkLab's groundbreaking research, Amanda invites us to stop viewing the disruptions of the hybrid age as problems to be solved and instead see them as signals to be heeded. She posits that Generation Z is a living prototype of our collective future. As the first true "digital natives," their instincts—for flexibility, for transparency, and for "intentional selfhood"—are not anomalies to be corrected, but indicators of evolving expectations of what we *all* need to thrive, today and tomorrow.

As you read the pages that follow, you will meet "Ryan," "Jenna," and "Marcus"—archetypes that illustrate the friction that occurs when old rules collide with new realities. Their stories challenge us to rethink familiar principles: the Golden Rule. We are taught to treat others as we wish to be treated, a noble sentiment that assumes our experience is universal. In a world of diverse minds, generations, and needs, this assumption creates invisible friction. The future of work asks us to evolve toward the "Platinum Rule"—treating others as *they* need to be treated. This isn't just about kindness, it is about the strategic empathy required to unlock potential in a workforce that no longer looks, thinks, or works the way we do *individually*. It is about building new systems that turn the hierarchy upside down to let wisdom flow in all directions.

This may not be a gentle process, but evolution isn't always gentle. This path demands that we look at "company-level non-negotiables" and ask if they serve the mission or merely the tradition. It demands that we recognize "grit" not as the ability to suffer in silence, but as the resilience to advocate for a way of working that honors our full humanity.

The future of work is not a destination. It is a reality we create with every decision and interaction. It is "phygital," it is fluid and it is deeply human. But to build, we must first be prepared to let go of the blueprints of the past. The question is not whether we need physical space, but whether we are bold enough to elevate its value (and reimagine its purpose) by treating it as a catalyst designed specifically for "human collisions"—generating the friction through purposeful connections and generating the creative energy to spark imagination that technology alone cannot replicate.

Legacy is comfortable, but evolution is necessary.

We must be willing to unlearn. The page is yours to turn.

Deborah Golden

Deloitte Consulting LLP | Global Executive in Innovation, Transformation, and Technology

TEDx Speaker & Catalyst for Unlearning

(Titles describe the roles, but impact defines the leader)

About Deloitte

Deloitte refers to one or more of Deloitte Touche Tohmatsu Limited, a UK private company limited by guarantee ("DTTL"), its network of member firms, and their related entities. DTTL and each of its member firms are legally separate and independent entities. DTTL (also referred to as "Deloitte Global") does not provide services to clients. In the United States, Deloitte refers to one or more of the US member firms of DTTL, their related entities that operate using the "Deloitte" name in the United States and their respective affiliates. Certain services may not be available to attest clients under the rules and regulations of public accounting. Please see www.deloitte.com/about to learn more about our global network of member firms.

Preface

WORK IS BROKEN. Gen Z can help us fix it. If we let them.

Now, you might shake your head or dismiss this as just another book that presents generational stereotypes as data. But let me tell you why this book is different:

- **I focus on business problems—not generational differences—first.** Many companies today are facing a threefold challenge: As hybrid work and globalization expand, they are struggling to connect people across more *generations* in the workplace than ever. With that comes an even wider range of *digital fluency* and (even if you're back in the office five days per week) a wider range of *geographies* as technology enables us to connect more offices across the world. This book digs into those challenges, but always with a primary focus on the business impact.
- **We look to generations as *prototypes,* not *stereotypes.*** Our research spans generations and locates trends in the data. As designers, when you prototype something, you keep what works and iterate on what doesn't. We have lots of ideas from Gen Z for you to try. But *you* get to pick what works best.

- **We share insights that can benefit *all* generations.** This is not a case of more seasoned folks giving up their preferences so that Gen Zers can get what they want in the workplace. Again, with the business impact in mind first, we looked for Gen Z ideas that could benefit *all*.

Even if you don't have a role to directly shape the future of work at your company, the clues from Gen Z are worth decoding. What we explore in this book is already influencing how work gets done—and because work is such a central part of life, the impact ripples far beyond the workplace. You may not like it, but understanding what's changing will give you leverage: helping you lead better, adapt faster, and stay effective as the unwritten norms evolve.

I run a company called ThinkLab, the research division of SANDOW Design Group and sister brand to well-known media brands like *Interior Design* magazine, *Metropolis, Design Milk, and more.* We've spent the past few years deeply researching Gen Z with the goal of understanding the future of work for those who are designing tomorrow's workspaces today. I've had hundreds of conversations with business leaders in our industry and beyond, looked at thousands of data points, and spent hours upon hours focus-grouping these topics.

You see, I work in an industry focused on designing and maximizing investments in physical space. We have been thinking about many of these ideas for a long time, especially since the workplace design sector is one of the largest in terms of design fees, as we've measured in our research on the *Interior Design* Giants of Design. (Think of this like *Fortune's* Fortune 500 list, but for Interior Design firms.) In recent years, people have become far more aware of how physical space affects how they work, think, and feel. The average person is suddenly engaged in conversations about the future of work, as well as the influence it has on their lives.

I have had my own struggles as a working mom, navigating a system that didn't feel built for me. I remember sitting at my desk one night, staring at an overflowing inbox and a work calendar that made no sense for the type of involved parent I wanted to be, totally overwhelmed. I had two competing thoughts running through my head: *"This isn't sustainable."* and *"Maybe it's just me?!"* (You can hear more about my story in my TED talk, "Work is Broken. Gen Z Can Help Fix It." You can find it at: https://www.ted.com/speakers/amanda_schneider or scan the QR code below.)

Watch Amanda's talk on TED.com here.

But I came to realize that people like me aren't the problem. The problem is our rules weren't built for the diversity of the modern workforce. Now, one thing about me: I have a natural bias toward action. Once I realize there's a problem, I cannot *not* act. And I wanted to fix this problem. (And I also want to recognize that there are those who face even greater challenges brought on by economic, cultural, and societal pressures that, due to my own invisible privilege, I don't experience.)

Ultimately, what surprised me most in the extensive research my team and I have done on Gen Zers was just how much their expectations echoed my own. Only they're articulating them earlier, louder, and with far less apology.

So, here are the three biggest things I've learned from Gen Z (Born 1997–2012) that can help attract *all* talent, including working parents, neurodiverse workers, and many other "others":

1. **They want flexibility.** Not just in where they work, but *when*. In fact, Future Forum research shows that most people actually prefer more flexibility in *when* they work, rather than *where* they work.
2. **They want transparency.** For Gen Zers, it's not just about pay. They want to know what's expected of them and what success (and work–life balance) really looks like at your company.

3. **They want impact.** Not just in words, but in the structures that allow their voices to shape the future—both the future of their company and of how work is done, as a whole.

What Gen Z is asking for isn't outlandish. In many cases, it's what, frankly, most of us have been craving all along. In some cases, it's what we've been *needing* all along.

When I couldn't find a workplace that worked for me, I built one. I started and scaled ThinkLab, eventually selling it to the largest media brand in our industry. (Post-acquisition, my team now runs the *Interior Design* Giants of Design study mentioned earlier.) Our model ended up working not just for moms, but for a wide variety of others. When we redesign how we think about some of these foundational structures and take on new perspectives, we can improve things for many.

It's no small task, and it can't be solved by design alone or policy alone. It requires rethinking our deepest assumptions about how work should work and for whom. The title of this book is *Work for What's Next,* which is what I hope you will join me in doing as you read this book.

Here's why the timing matters: The pace of change has never been faster. If we don't rethink work now, we risk locking in the same, outdated defaults just as the next era of business—one increasingly powered by AI—is being defined. We often worry—and rightly so—that AI is biased. But AI is only as biased as the people who train it. Until we correct our assumptions, we'll keep building systems, both digital and human, that reflect those same defaults.

To move through this transition, we don't need more policies that patch up old problems. We need fresh inputs, new *prototypes,* and the courage to try things we haven't tried before.

The risk of staying stuck isn't neutral—it's costly. The cost of waiting is already showing up in burnout, turnover, and missed opportunities for innovation. Companies that fail to adapt are seeing younger talent opt out, mid-career employees burn out, and competitors move faster because their systems are better built for speed, adaptability, and attracting the right talent. In an AI-fueled, globalized market, organizations that cling to old norms won't just feel like they're behind; they'll become irrelevant.

That's why this book looks to Gen Z. Not because older generations have nothing to offer, or because younger ones "deserve" special treatment. It's because Gen Z professionals bring a perspective no one else can. Gen Z is the first generation to grow up fully digital-first. The oldest of the group graduated from college in 2019, and none of them knew the workplace as it was before hybrid work took over. They don't carry the same assumptions many of us do, which makes them unusually good at spotting when the old rules no longer fit. It's similar to how best-selling author Adam Grant describes "*vuja de*" moments (which is the opposite of *déjà vu*): taking a look at a problem we've seen a thousand times but with fresh eyes.

This book is for leaders, teams, and organizations who are tired of spinning in the same debates—remote vs. in-office, perks vs. pay, tradition vs. disruption—and are ready for new playbooks.

Part I reveals groundbreaking research on how trust and communication at work is breaking down—and why those shifts matter.

Part II covers foundational concepts that redefine what "better work" means—showing how personal clarity, reimagined leadership, and new cultural signals are transforming how, where, and why we work.

Part III will help you reframe the challenges of work through 10 key shifts. Whether you're a CEO, a manager, an HR leader, or an individual trying to navigate your own career, each chapter unpacks a deeply researched prototype—informed by ThinkLab's Gen Z advisory board, influenced by experts on our *Design Nerds Anonymous* podcast, and proven by our deep qualitative and quantitative studies—that all point to clues for a better way forward.

We'll explore solutions to the following business challenges:

- **Trust and connection:** how to rebuild credibility and belonging when digital body language has replaced many hallway conversations.
- **Recruitment and retention:** why the hiring process feels broken—and how to design it to build trust from day one.
- **Culture and purpose:** how to move from lofty mission statements to lived daily practices.
- **Collaboration and communication:** how to balance individual work and group time, communicate to avoid decision gridlock, and build systems that actually move work forward.

- **Mentorship and learning:** why the old apprenticeship model is evolving, and how digital-first mentorship and continuous learning can help teams keep pace with rapid change.

Across these shifts runs one big throughline: Work isn't just something to survive. It should be something that works—both for companies *and* for people. By rethinking old assumptions and experimenting with better models, we can design workplaces that unlock potential instead of draining it, and drive bigger business impact in the process.

So, as you read, I invite you to pause and ask yourself: "Are we designing work for yesterday's assumptions or for tomorrow's talent?" Because ironically, even as we free people from coming into a physical office every day, in some ways we've put even more pressure on the workplace: to foster connection, reflect our values, and justify us showing up. But even the best designed offices can't fix today's challenges alone.

The future of work will be defined by those willing to build what's next. If we listen and learn from these shifts, we won't just reimagine work for one generation. We'll build workplaces and workflows that work for everyone. More importantly, I want them to work for my kids and (hopefully, someday) my grandkids.

I hope you enjoy this book, but above all, I hope it inspires change for the better for you personally and for your organization. And if there's a story you'd like to share, reach out to me on LinkedIn (@amandajeanschneider). I'd love to hear it, and who knows? Maybe you'll find yourself on the *Design Nerds Anonymous* podcast to tell it.

Connect with Amanda on LinkedIn here.

PART

I

How We Got Here

IF YOU'VE EVER looked up from your computer and thought, *why do we still work like this?*—you're not alone.

Or maybe you're a leader who knows there's no going back, sees that this moment isn't working, and is determined to shape what's next.

You're not imagining it—the problem runs deeper than leadership styles or company policies.

The systems shaping modern work were built for a world that no longer exists. The nine-to-five schedule? Born from the logic of the assembly line. Summers off from school? A relic of the harvest season, when kids were needed in the fields. Even the idea of "climbing the ladder" came from an era when most workers expected a single employer, a single path, and a single measure of success. None of these norms were designed for today's world of knowledge work—and yet, we continue to organize our lives around them.

Those rules made sense once. But today's world runs on something entirely different. Knowledge work happens everywhere and nowhere—across time zones, devices, and disciplines. The workforce is more diverse than ever, and technology is moving faster than our culture can adapt. Yet we still measure performance by outdated standards that no longer fit today's reality. The game has changed, but we're still playing by old rules.

That's what this first section is here to explore: the urgency of this moment, the cultural habits we've outgrown, and the patterns we need to name before we can change them. Because before we can design a better way forward, we must first understand why, exactly, work isn't working today.

By the end of this section, you won't be able to unsee the patterns holding us back—or stop imagining what comes next.

1

The Trust Gap No One Saw Coming

The big idea: Professionals are experiencing an erosion of trust with their colleagues. This growing trust gap is driven by miscommunication across generations, geographies, and levels of digital fluency. It's more than a business problem—it's a cultural one.

IN THE PAST few years, the workplace has evolved. In fact, it had a full-blown identity crisis. One minute, we were printing meeting agendas, leaving voicemails, and clocking out at 5 p.m. The next, we're juggling 10 Slack channels, 6 hours of Zoom calls, and a calendar that starts before coffee and ends, well, never?

The transition to hybrid work was already underway, but the COVID-19 pandemic acted as both an accelerant and a complicating force. What might have previously taken a decade unfolded in just a few years, and culturally, we are still playing catch up. Before remote work surged in 2020, less than 5 percent of the U.S. workforce worked remotely three or more days per week.[1] By 2022, nearly half (49 percent) of global desk workers were operating in a hybrid arrangement.[2] And as of 2025, flexible work policies remain a top priority: 40 percent of U.S. hybrid and remote employees surveyed said they would start to look for another job

3

if they could no longer choose when and where to work.[3] This marks a dramatic shift and signals that is not just a temporary adjustment but a fundamental, lasting transformation in how and where work happens.

Gallup's 2025 workplace report opens with the stark question: "Is the global workplace at a breaking point?"[4] The data suggests we may be approaching one. In 2024, global employee engagement fell sharply compared to the previous year. This was the only measured decline in the past 12 years, with one exception: the similar drop in 2020. Gallup estimates that the 2024 engagement drop alone cost the global economy $438 billion in lost productivity.

The message is clear: while organizations successfully pivoted to hybrid work, many are now confronting a second cliff—evidence that the model, in its current form, is faltering. If the first wave was about reacting to crisis, this next phase demands intentional redesign.

For so long, knowledge work relied on norms that were largely unwritten. But hybrid work, asynchronous tools, and a multigenerational workforce have scrambled the signals.

Now, things that once seemed obvious—how to show up, how to communicate, how to build trust—have become open-ended questions, without clear answers or consensus: Some professionals prefer structure. Others lean into flexibility and feedback in real time. Some crave structure, while others value autonomy. The end result is often disconnection. According to Gallup's research on hybrid work, some of the most commonly cited disadvantages include a weaker connection to company culture, decreased collaboration, impaired working relationships with coworkers, and reduced cross-functional communication and collaboration.[5]

In other words, everyone is trying their best, but things still get missed. Messages are misunderstood. Connection is harder to come by than it should be.

The truth is: This isn't anyone's fault. But it is everyone's *problem*.

By looking more deeply at these daily disconnects, we can come closer to a solution. A hidden code that holds the key to how we work, lead, and relate to each other. Once we learn how to crack that code, we don't just communicate better. We build stronger teams, deeper trust, and a more human way of working.

That's what this book is here to help you do.

At ThinkLab, we sit at the intersection of interior design, media, and research on the built environment. That means my team and I have a rare, 360-degree view of how economic, cultural, and technological shifts affect the spaces where people not only work, but live, learn, heal, and more. As ThinkLab's founder and president, I directed its 2023 generational research study[6] and follow-up work[7] in 2024 and 2025 to develop a radically different approach from traditional studies in this area.

The insights shared here are not theoretical—they are drawn from the very decision-makers who influence the spending of billions of dollars in real-world projects that are built every year. Our research is distilled into actionable guidance for leaders who want to move faster, retain talent, and create environments built for what's next.

To show what I mean, let's start with a quick game of *Would You Rather*. Play along by answering this question:

Would you rather:

(a) stay in the same job you're in now for the rest of your career?
(b) change jobs every year until you retire?

When we pose this question to multigenerational audiences, the majority choose (a) staying put. But when we ask predominantly Gen Z groups, the overwhelming choice is (b) changing jobs every year.

"Gen Z just lacks loyalty," you might be thinking. And you would not be alone in thinking so. (In fact, I will tackle this perception of a "lack of loyalty" among Gen Zers in Chapter 9.) But in ThinkLab's research, Gen Z respondents explained their reasoning differently: "I'd rather build skills through diverse experiences." And even, "If I were hiring, I'd want someone who brings the rich experiences of multiple companies to my brand."

This simple question reveals just how differently each generation views growth, loyalty, and the very idea of career success. It also shows why generational research matters. The goal is not to determine whether one group is right or wrong. It is about recognizing how shifts in perception across *all* generations can help us spot early signals about where the future of work is going—and give us tools for open dialogue within our teams.

Why This Shift Runs Deeper Than Past Generational Tensions

At first glance, you might consider these answers as simply an example of a typical generational difference. After all, tension between age groups is hardly new. Baby Boomers were criticized by their elders for the "radical" ideas and shifting values they championed when they entered the workforce. Every generation has faced skepticism from the one before it. Some may even argue that these challenges are related to life stage and were no different for previous generations at the same age.

But today's divide is different—not just because of *what* we disagree on but because the world around us is shifting faster than our ability to adapt. The gap is widening. Here's why:

- **Hybrid work has upended the old playbook.** For many, the 9-to-5, office-only model no longer works the way it used to, but there is no general consensus on what works better.
- **Technology is racing ahead, but culture is lagging behind.** We're armed with new digital tools, yet many are still clunky, awkward, and disconnected from how people naturally work.
- **Multiple generations are now navigating the same workplace but using entirely different mental operating systems.** Simply due to their lived experiences, Gen Zers operate with innately digital reflexes, while older colleagues naturally rely on analog instincts.
- **Geography is no longer a boundary.** Technology has enabled instant collaboration across continents. But without in-person connection, trust remains hard to build.
- **Work is no longer confined to a set time or place.** Burdened with constant pings, countless avenues for communication (email, text, calls, Slack, etc.), and blurred work–life boundaries, our attention is fragmented, and our focus is fraying.

What we're dealing with isn't just a culture clash or a difference in preferences. It's something deeper. It's a breakdown of trust in each other. And that breakdown is slowing performance, stalling innovation, and quietly eroding the foundation of effective teams. Without trust, communication falters. Collaboration becomes cautious, and we all take fewer and fewer risks.

Generational research from ThinkLab brings this tension into focus. When asked, "What is the hardest part about working in a hybrid world?" Gen Z respondents are nearly twice as likely as Boomers to say "Nothing, hybrid is awesome" (Figure 1.1). On the surface, they sound optimistic. But dig a little deeper, and you'll see cracks. Twenty-four percent of Gen Zers also indicate that *trust* is their biggest challenge with hybrid work. That's twice the percentage of Boomers who said the same.

In other words, younger workers may feel at ease navigating the tools and flexibility of hybrid work, but that doesn't mean they know how to build relationships from behind their screens—or that they feel secure in those relationships. Trust between colleagues—once developed through casual hallway chats and shared routines—now requires

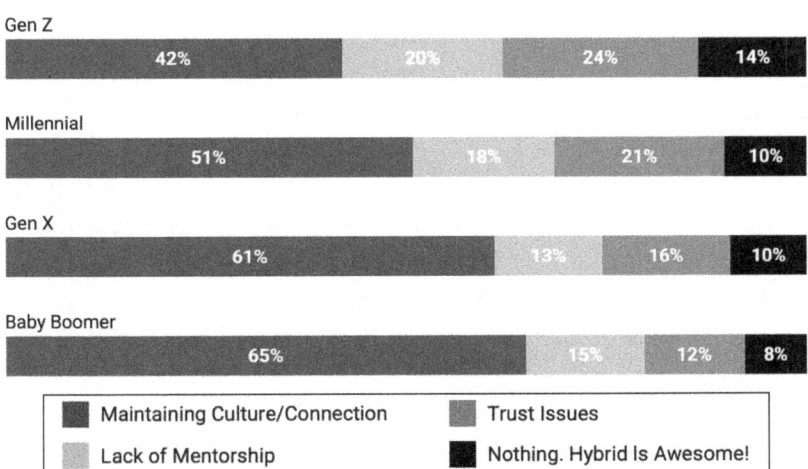

WHAT IS THE HARDEST PART ABOUT WORKING IN A HYBRID WORLD?

Gen Z
42% | 20% | 24% | 14%

Millennial
51% | 18% | 21% | 10%

Gen X
61% | 13% | 16% | 10%

Baby Boomer
65% | 15% | 12% | 8%

- Maintaining Culture/Connection
- Trust Issues
- Lack of Mentorship
- Nothing. Hybrid Is Awesome!

Figure 1.1   **Gen Z respondents are twice as likely as boomers to cite trust as their biggest hybrid-work challenge.**

Source: ThinkLab.design Gen Z research / with permission of ThinkLab.

more intention to build, and more skill to sustain. When that trust is missing, even the brightest teams with the best tools struggle to move forward.

You may be thinking, "The problem is hybrid work. We should just go back to the office." But the truth is we can't put that toothpaste back in the tube. Technology isn't going backward. The path forward lies in finding new ways to close this gap, together. It is about using generational signals to understand what is changing beneath the surface and figure out how to navigate it.

The Trust Gap: Three Real Stories

Today's workplace is shaped by a collision of expectations. What one person sees as taking advantage of a flexible schedule, another sees as disengagement. What seems like clear communication to some feels incomplete or invisible to others.

While these gaps often show up as generational tension, the reality is more complex. They are also the product of asynchronous work, fractured communication channels, and a shrinking window of time for building trust as work has less face-to-face time. Whether it's a recent grad on Zoom calls from an office full of headphones, a remote engineer navigating blurred boundaries, or a seasoned sales leader losing face time with once-loyal clients—the disconnects are real, and they affect everyone.

These three stories are inspired by real experiences inside companies trying to make hybrid work, well, work. Together, they reveal how misunderstanding each other isn't just a side effect of modern changes to how we work. It's a business risk hiding in plain sight.

Story #1: "The In-Office Zoom"

Meet Ryan, a Gen Z marketing analyst who recently joined a consulting firm. On day one, he was told the company valued in-person connection, so he'd be expected in the office most days. His manager, Steve, was direct: "We need face time. Collaboration is better in person."

So, Ryan shows up. Within ten minutes, his schedule kicks off. It's a back-to-back slog of video calls with clients and project team members in other cities. At lunch, Ryan walks past Steve's office. It's empty. Steve is traveling for client meetings in Houston that day and neglected to mention it.

The irony isn't lost on Ryan. Although *he* had followed the rules of in-person attendance, the logic didn't follow him. The physical office was supposed to spark connection. Instead, it feels like a quieter version of his own apartment, just with worse snacks and less control.

What Ryan doesn't yet understand is that Steve is managing across three time zones, preparing for a virtual sales pitch, and coordinating updates with a regional team. The misalignment wasn't intentional, just uncoordinated. But to Ryan, commuting into the office only to spend hours on virtual calls feels like a bait and switch.

This sort of disconnection affects professionals of every generation, and it's the result of structural blind spots in their organizations.

Story #2: "Muted, Misread, and Missing the Mark"

Now meet Jenna, a Gen Z analyst working remotely for a large consumer brand. Things seem to be going well. She's meeting deadlines, attending calls, and even joining in the team's online "watercooler" chat about weekend plans. She works from a shared apartment with three roommates, often bouncing between her bedroom, the kitchen table, and a local coffee shop, just to find some quiet and a stable internet connection.

Her coworkers, mostly in their thirties and forties, seem to be juggling a lot: children, home renovations, midday tax appointments. Jenna watches them log on from the sidelines of soccer games, waiting rooms, and living rooms in mid-chaos. She figures that if her colleagues can take a call from their SUVs, it must be fine for her to teach a midday yoga class on Thursdays. As long as the work gets done, right?

So, it hits hard when her manager schedules a call to say she's being placed on a performance improvement plan for "poor communication and inconsistent availability." Jenna is blindsided.

What confuses her most is that other team members also adjust their schedules to fulfill personal obligations. One analyst often takes meetings from her car between daycare pickups. A senior strategist has his video availability turned off for half the day. But no one ever said those things were a problem as far as Jenna knows.

The issue isn't that Jenna is slacking. It's that the boundaries around professionalism are shifting, and no one is drawing the lines clearly. Expectations have become implicit, unevenly enforced, and shaped more by perception than by policy.

Story #3: "From Hugs and Handshakes to Drive-Bys"

Meet Marcus, a Gen X senior sales rep for a commercial furniture brand. He's spent more than 20 years building strong relationships with architects and interior designers who recommend his product for their large workplace projects. His job has always been about trust: showing up, asking the right questions, and using a consultative back-and-forth approach that helps clients envision the perfect solution before they can even verbalize what they need.

It used to work. Every month, he would host a standing meeting in the firm materials library for an hour-long presentation. As long as he brought great food, the entire workplace design team would show up.

Now, those meetings are gone. They've been replaced by 15-minute walkthroughs. Instead of a full hour to connect with the whole group, he gets a calendar hold labeled "Vendor Day" with six other companies slotted back-to-back.

He tries to follow up with digital materials: a personalized video walkthrough, a Miro board with inspirational images of new product launches, a PDF brochure attachment. But weeks pass without any replies. And when he finally hears back, it's often to say they've moved ahead with someone else.

Marcus isn't falling behind because he's unwilling to change. He's falling behind because the rules of engagement have changed faster than he has been able to acknowledge them. No one has the time to slow down long enough to see what's missing or what the implications will be.

The Common Thread: Mismatched Expectations in a Shifting System

Ryan, Jenna, and Marcus may come from different generations, industries, and roles, but their stories share a common root. Each of them was working hard to do the "right" thing, only to realize that the rules had changed—or worse, were never clearly stated to begin with.

Ryan showed up to the office in person, only to find collaboration happening primarily online. Jenna took advantage of her job's flexible hours, only to be called unreliable. Marcus relied on trust and face time, only to discover those human touchpoints had been mostly replaced by fast-moving digital communication or drive-by exchanges. What they experienced wasn't failure. It was friction born from a lack of *shared* expectations, stretched across time zones, tech stacks, and generational habits.

What Ryan, Jenna, and Marcus experienced—the confusion, frustration, and quiet shame—is not uncommon. And right now, many employees, managers, and even senior leaders are operating in that same fog.

The solution is more clarity. Before we solve for performance, or culture, or retention, we need to engage in more intentional conversations about what good work looks like in this new context. We have to rebuild trust in each other—across offices, across tools, and across generations.

So What? Key Takeaways from Chapter 1

- **Today's workplace isn't broken because of where we work.** It's broken because we've stopped being clear about how we work together.
- **Generational research can reveal how differently we interpret trust, loyalty, and success.** But those differences are amplified by geography, digital fluency, and communication habits.
- **Hybrid and digital tools didn't cause the disconnect.** They exposed how fragile our systems of alignment already were. It's no one's *fault*, but it's everyone's *problem*.
- **Most breakdowns at work aren't about skill, effort, or ill intention.** They stem from unspoken rules and misaligned expectations.
- **Reduced face time and compressed communication windows mean trust has to be built faster, with fewer touchpoints.** And that's a strategic challenge, not just a generational one.
- **If we want to rebuild trust, we have to stop assuming alignment and start designing it.** That means clarifying expectations, naming assumptions, and building systems that support shared understanding.

2

Shift Happens: Why the Time to Rethink Everything Is Now

The big idea: The unspoken norms shaping how we work were built for a world that no longer exists. If we don't pause to question the rules we've inherited, we'll keep reinforcing the very problems we're trying to solve.

EVERYONE FEELS RELENTLESSLY busy. But is anyone getting anywhere?

That's the quiet question humming beneath today's frenzied work culture. Employees are overwhelmed. Leaders are skeptical. And productivity, once easy to measure, is now nearly impossible to define.

Email was once expected to make knowledge work more efficient, but today, it's adding to the noise. The average employee spends 34 percent of their time on email and chat.[1] The use of AI-based tools is surging, as workers chase similar promises of improved efficiency and higher productivity. But the question remains: Will these tools reduce stress and workload, or just accelerate the pace of busyness?

We Must See the Disconnect to Fix It

Professionals are grappling with uncertainty in workplaces everywhere, and the data proves it.

Diving deeper into Gallup's latest workplace report mentioned in the previous chapter, the sharpest declines in engagement are happening where it matters most—among managers. Overall, manager engagement dropped from 30 percent in 2024 to 27 percent in 2025, with even steeper declines among young (under 35) and female managers.[2] Engagement among individual contributors remained flat at just 18 percent.

These numbers reflect more than fatigue. They point to a system under strain after years of disruption, digital transformation, and shifting employee expectations around flexibility. The old rules for leading, measuring, and connecting no longer match the messy reality of modern knowledge work.

With this in mind, let's play another game.

Would you rather:

(a) go back to a world where you knew how to win, even if it means mistaking tradition for wisdom and missing opportunities to evolve?

(b) get dragged into a future with no rules, just noise, speed, and a constant fear that you're already behind?

That's the real choice leaders face today. Not remote vs. office. Not digital vs. human. But, instead: Certainty vs. chaos. Familiar dysfunction vs. disorienting change.

The question isn't *if* the world has changed. It's *what do we do now?*

The Old Rules That Still Define Work

How can leaders make this choice? How can they navigate this conflict? Take a page from a common approach to counseling. When working through difficult feelings, "you have to name it to tame it." Perhaps this approach applies here, too. So, let's start by naming the unwritten rules of knowledge work and tracing where they came from, so that we can begin to explore where they are headed next.

First, let's think back to the unwritten rules followed by most companies pre-2019, and consider which still apply to your workplace today:

1. **Work is physical: It has a set time and place.**
   The workday runs from 9 to 5 (roughly) and is anchored in a physical office. Showing up is an indicator of contribution.
2. **Trust in management is expected.**
   Strong leadership means projecting confidence and certainty, not curiosity or vulnerability.
3. **Recruiting is targeted: Companies focus on filling open, full-time roles.**
   Hiring focuses on matching résumés to requirements. A typical interview process naturally hinges on a candidate's experience, surface-level likability, and perceived interpersonal fit with the team.
4. **Loyalty means employees prove commitment through years of service.**
   Retaining talent means offering stability. Employees stay, grow, and retire at the same company. They prove their commitment through years of service, and job-hopping signals instability and can raise concerns about an employee's reliability.
5. **Culture is synonymous with the office.**
   Fostering team connection, collaboration, and trust relies on the informal, day-to-day interactions that happen when people share the same physical space. Belonging is built through proximity: the hallway hellos, the coffee catch-ups, the chance encounters that come with working side by side.
6. **Careers are cumulative: Time invested equals a step up the ladder.**
   Advancement tends to follow a steady, vertical path, where experience is generally valued over experimentation.
7. **Collaboration is centered on synchronous time.**
   Face-to-face conversations are the default mode for collaboration at work: sharing updates, aligning decisions, and showing progress. In-person meetings are considered markers of progress.
8. **Communication is top-down and analog-first.**
   Leaders act as messengers, filtering information and sharing what they believe employees need to know. The strongest messages are thorough and detailed. The best communication happens face-to-face.

9. **Mentorship happens through osmosis.**
   Built on an apprenticeship model where skills were developed by observing more-experienced workers, mentorship relies on in-person proximity to leaders. Guidance flows one way—older to younger—and generally stays within the walls of a single company.

10. **Learning is an event. The goal is memorization.**
   Think about the last corporate training session you attended. Did you take part in structured sessions, courses, or materials delivered from the company to the employee through a trainer? Learning is often treated as a scheduled event, imparted in a classroom setting with an emphasis on memorization.

Activity: What's a Rule You Inherited That's Not on This List, But Still Shapes How You "Show Up" to Work Today?

Maybe it's a rule defining what counts as success. Maybe it's about who gets to speak up. (Or who doesn't.) Maybe it's about when it's considered OK to rest.

Take a moment to name it. Write it down. Just start by noticing it.

Why the Old Rules Are Failing All of Us

The rules that still shape how we "show up" to work weren't designed for today's world—they were built for a time when work looked completely different.

Let's start by defining knowledge work: the segment of the workforce that is the focus of this book. Knowledge work refers to jobs that only generate value through information, analysis, and problem-solving rather than physical labor.

Knowledge work as we know it emerged only after the industrial revolution, a period when most jobs had to be performed at a set time and location, as with assembly lines. At that time, the majority of employees were men, often supported by full-time caregivers at home.

This system assumed stable, single-income households, predictable 9-to-5 schedules, and a consistent physical presence in the office. These rules suited a world with clear lines separating home and work— and fewer expectations of balancing the two. What worked then is working against us now.

For example, many of the unwritten rules we've inherited are rooted in historically masculine ideals that prioritized stoicism over vulnerability, competition (even dominance) over collaboration, self-reliance over support, and a mental toughness that came with *just pushing through*.[3] According to the CDC, the suicide rate among men in the United States is nearly four times higher than that of women, and rates of depression and burnout in working-age men continue to rise.[4] Put simply, these rules aren't working for men anymore.

At the same time, women continue to face their own distinct set of pressures. Despite recent progress, they continue to shoulder a disproportionate share of caregiving and household responsibilities. A 2024 study by the Gender Equity Policy Institute found that in the United States, working women still spend twice as many hours per week as working men on childcare and domestic tasks.[5]

And that's just scratching the surface. The numbers show what many already feel: Not everyone is carrying the same load. For people of color, it often means battling systemic barriers and microaggressions that compound daily stress. For lower-income workers, it's the reality of fewer buffers and higher stakes when disruption hits. (And, of course, many people fall into more than one of these groups.)

Simply put: The old rules don't meet the moment. The context has now shifted.

Still, even as those systems falter, new ones have yet to fully take shape. We are living in-between, caught between outdated expectations and an uncertain path ahead. And being in that space is uncomfortable, disorienting, and often exhausting.

But opportunities like these come along rarely.

Seeing Disruption as a Clue, Not Just a Crisis

We were already on the path to digitization, disruption, and rethinking work, but the 2020 global pandemic threw things into overdrive.

It sped up the path we were already on, showing us a future we weren't ready for, and didn't like. It exposed just how fragile our systems really are. And in that disruption, we have the opportunity to see both the cracks and the potential, *if* we take this moment and learn from it.

Activity: Capture Your "What's the Point?" Moment

I invite you to think back to a time during the past 10 years when something about work or life suddenly didn't make sense anymore. Maybe a rule that used to feel normal stopped feeling right. Maybe seeing your days reduced to a grid of Zoom calls made you question whether any of it was actually effective. Maybe working remotely made putting on that tie in the morning seem unnecessary. Or maybe getting to take a 10-minute break to get your daughter off the bus made that commute seem less worthwhile.

Pick your own moment of clarity, and record it in a notebook, in your Notes app, or by any other method you choose. That moment may hold a clue about what needs to change, whether for you or your organization. (If this idea resonates, you can hear more about my what's the point moment in my TED talk, "Work is Broken. Gen Z Can Help Fix It."[6] You can find it at: https://www.ted.com/speakers/amanda_schneider.)

Watch Amanda's talk on TED.com here.

If the old rules no longer serve us, and the new ones haven't fully arrived, the question is: What comes next, and how do we get there?

We would likely not have drafted the unwritten norms of work this way if we were starting fresh today. The discomfort is cross-generational, and the patterns are clear in the data. People of all ages are starting to ask deeper questions about how we measure impact, what we value in leadership, and what work should really look and feel like.

Defining the New Rules of Knowledge Work

We aren't tracking simply abstract ideas. These are patterns we are already seeing in motion. The following "new rules" reflect where high-performing teams are headed. Throughout the rest of this book, we will show how these patterns emerged and how you can capitalize on them.

1. **Work is phygital (physical + digital = phygital): Digital sparks connection; face-to-face makes it stick.**
   Time and place are tools, not rules. The strongest teams use digital to enable access and efficiency and in-person moments to deepen trust, culture, and belonging.

2. **Trust is something cocreated between employer, employee, and coworkers.**
   Authenticity has become the new authority. Trust grows when a company is clear about what it stands for, consistent in how it shows up online and in person, and courageous enough to invite others into the process.

3. **Recruiting is dynamic: Companies match talent for now, *and* for what's next.**
   Companies are thinking critically about what AI can do, what's best handled by contractors, and when it's worth investing in full-time talent. The goal is to match opportunity both with a company's priorities and where a candidate is in their journey— whether it's for a reason, a season, or a long-term path.

4. **Loyalty flows both ways: Careers are built in chapters, not lifetimes.**
   In a world of endless options and access to information, loyalty isn't about staying put. It's about staying aligned. The question

isn't "Why are they *leaving?*" It's "Why should they *stay?*" People stay where they grow—and leave when their growth stalls.

5. **Culture grows in microcultures.**

   It isn't anchored to a single building or even a single team, but to the small, closer-knit tribes that form within and across organizations. These microcultures are built on intentional norms, shared rituals, and mutual respect, whether they happen in an office, across time zones, or in digital spaces.

6. **Careers are nonlinear: Growth isn't just up. It can be deep, broad, or both.**

   People move fluidly between roles, projects, and employment structures, guided by fit more than by status. The most successful individuals aren't found climbing a predefined ladder. Instead, they're motivated by personal curiosity and by companies that value and reward their uniquely developed strengths.

7. **Collaboration is fluid: Synchronous when it matters, async when it helps.**

   High-performing teams don't default to meetings; they align their objective with the right format. In-person (synchronous) time is used for work that benefits from real-time energy, such as making critical decisions. Asynchronous tools support focus, enable participation across locations, and increase efficiency. (Note: Async means there's a delay when a message is sent and when it is received, allowing for responses at a different time.)

8. **Communication is customized and scalable.**

   Clarity matters more than volume. In a world of ever-larger project teams and shrinking attention spans, the most impactful leaders act as multipliers, crafting messages that capture attention and can be carried forward by others.

9. **Mentorship is accessible to all.**

   It blends in-person and digital connection, flows across generations in every direction, and recognizes that no one holds all the answers. The strongest systems link people to peers, leaders, and external networks, making mentorship more inclusive, flexible, and sustainable.

10. Learning is a mindset. The goal is curiosity.

Upskilling is no longer about memorizing facts. In the AI era, it means asking better questions and knowing how to access the right tools, people, and ideas when they're needed. The most effective professionals don't wait for company training. They take ownership of their growth, using every available resource to build skills aligned with their unique career path.

We now know why the time to rethink work is now. We have named the old rules and defined new ones to reflect how work is changing across generations. But before we can apply these ideas at scale in Part III, we need to pause and look inward. We can't really design better work without identifying what "better" means, so in Part II we'll cover foundational concepts that show how personal clarity, reimagined leadership, and new cultural signals are transforming how, where, and why we work.

So What? Key Takeaways from Chapter 2

- **The way we measure knowledge work hasn't kept pace with how work actually happens today.** Technology and hybrid work have changed the context around how work gets done, yet our unwritten norms around work have not kept pace.
- **Outdated rules still shape how we "show up," even if we no longer believe in them.** In order to change them, we first have to identify them.
- **These inherited systems weren't built for our current lives,** and they are failing all of us, across generations and identities.
- **The discomfort many are feeling is a sign that we're in a moment of transition, not just dysfunction.** A better reality is ahead if we make intentional changes now.
- **The future of knowledge work isn't arriving all at once.** It's being shaped in real time by those bold enough to question the status quo and redefine it.

PART

II

Foundational Concepts

SEEING WHAT'S BROKEN is only the first step. The harder work begins when we decide to do something about it.

Before we can rebuild the way we work, we have to understand the foundations that make progress possible—starting with people, then organizations, then the systems that connect them.

Because transformation doesn't happen through new policies alone. It happens when individuals get clear on what they need to do their best work, when organizations align around purpose instead of habit, and when structures are designed to listen, learn, and adapt.

In the chapters ahead, we'll explore three core ideas that set the stage for every shift that follows:

- **The Individual (Chapter 3):** How self-awareness and clarity unlock performance and well-being.
- **The Organization (Chapter 4):** Why designing for people—not just process—creates stronger, more resilient cultures.
- **The System (Chapter 5):** How new models like shadow boards and cross-generational forums give every voice a place in shaping what comes next.

This is the groundwork for lasting momentum—the human and structural alignment that allows the next 10 shifts to take root.

By the end of this section, you'll see where meaningful change begins—and how to build the foundation strong enough to sustain it.

3

The Era of Intentional Selfhood: Why It All Starts with Us

> **The big idea:** Before we can redesign knowledge work for the better, we must redefine what *better* means. Most of us spent years in 9-to-5 office jobs without asking when, where, or what makes us most productive. Take the time to identify those preferences and trade-offs. Clarity with ourselves is the first step to reshaping better work lives.

WHAT IS THE first stereotype that comes to mind when you think of Gen Zers?

Maybe you've heard they lack a work ethic.

Maybe you've questioned their sense of professionalism.

Maybe you've said (or at least thought) that they seem self-centered or even entitled.

These are common critiques leveled at this new generation that now makes up nearly 18 percent of the U.S. workforce,[1] with near-term projections of 30 percent by 2030.[2] What if they have something to teach us, simply because they're looking at the world through a different lens?

What Gen Z Can Teach Others

While most of this book is for leaders, this chapter is for the individual worker. I invite you (and your employees, colleagues, and friends) to step into Gen Z's perspective—not to critique it, but to learn from it. If you can't beat them, join them, right? It's easy to dismiss this generation as self-centered, but the truth is today we *all* live in a world designed around personalization. Tailored ads, curated feeds, and customized recommendations have taught all of us to expect experiences that reflect our preferences. Gen Z just grew up with that expectation baked in.

Gen Z author Hannah Grady Williams has explained that she and her peers create their own personal brands as kids, which they then carry into their work lives. As she writes in *A Leader's Guide to Unlocking Gen Z*, "We've already had our own brand—what I call the 'NarcisStory'—by the time you hire us."[3]

Williams defines the "NarcisStory" as the personal narrative each Gen Zer is building—a reputation shaped by their interests, activities, and the image they want to project. Most Gen Zers expect work and every other choice they make in their life to align with that authentic vision of themselves.

Gen Zers might have first developed their personal brands to connect with their digital followers, but for them, these public perceptions don't stay online. Their brand isn't just about how they're perceived—it informs how they live. It's why they care where their coffee comes from, what their employer stands for, and whether their daily work aligns with their personal values. And understanding this mindset is key: As Williams points out, if you don't recognize how central the NarcisStory is to Gen Z's identity, you risk missing out on its talent entirely.

To get the best from Gen Zers, we have to understand what makes them tick. But perhaps to get the best from *ourselves*—as leaders, teammates, or individuals—we need to understand what makes *us* tick, too.

Because here's the twist: We all have personal brands. Gen Zers just build theirs with intention. The rest of us might be building ours by accident.

Maybe Gen Z Is Just Saying What We Are All Thinking

When you really look at what Gen Z wants from work, it's not so different from what many of us want, too. At least according to Deloitte Global's 2025 survey of more than 14,000 Gen Z respondents worldwide.[4]

This annual survey, now in its 14th year, consistently finds that Gen Z prioritizes:

- **Work–life balance**
- **Learning and development**
- **Purpose and well-being alongside financial compensation**
- **Guidance and mentorship**—not just task oversight—from managers

Most of us want *all* of these things, too. But here's the part we don't talk about enough: *How* we get those things—work–life balance, purpose, mentorship—isn't abstract. It's in the details. It's in how we communicate with our team, choose our projects, set our boundaries, define success, and structure our day. When people understand themselves better—that's when real breakthroughs become possible.

A Better Future of Work Starts with You

As we move forward, we will explore how understanding our own preferences—including when we work best, where we feel most focused, and what trade-offs we are willing to make—can help shape a more flexible and fulfilling future of knowledge work.

Just as importantly, in the next chapter, we will consider how organizations can do the same. In a world where one size no longer fits all, the most successful matches between employer and employee stem from both sides being honest about what they need, what they are willing to give up, and what they are not willing to give up. And most often, it's not a matter of unwillingness—it's that many haven't identified those needs in the first place.

When I was preparing my TEDx talk, I sent a rough recording to my best friend, Beth. One line in the early draft read, "The future of work starts with sharing when and where we work best." After listening, she gently pushed back. She said, "Amanda, you've been thinking about this for years because of the industry you work in. But honestly, I've never once stopped to ask myself that. I just went to the office because that's what you do."

With that comment I realized that while I had spent years blogging about the future of work, thinking about what engages people in today's workplaces, building a company around my own needs as a working mom, and guiding consultants into more flexible ways of working, most people have not had the unspoken permission to think about work this way. Her own experience—and, likely, that of many knowledge workers—has been focused on getting through her usual responsibilities, without looking at the bigger picture and considering what could be improved in her working life.

Define What "Better" Looks Like

Like Beth, most of us have never been asked to define what "better" means when it comes to work. We just assumed work was something we had to do or perhaps a place we had to go, because that's how the system was built.

But what if we dropped that assumption? In fact, imagine every *new* rule in Chapter 2 was already true for you: You don't have to be physically present in the office from 9 to 5 every day. You don't have to mold your life around your job. Instead, imagine your job could be molded around *you*.

How I Defined What "Better" Looks Like for Me

Let's start with a bit of my story: I left the traditional working world because it stopped working for me. Like many couples, my husband and I couldn't make two full-time jobs and a young family fit together. Most of my paycheck was going to daycare costs. When we found out we were expecting our second son, we notified the daycare before we even called our parents. Even with sibling priority, we were told he wouldn't have a spot until he was seven months old. I was also growing more frustrated with the daily routine. I was literally waking my kids up to rush them to daycare, only to rush them home after work and put them to bed. Ironically, in working so hard to provide for my kids, I was actually missing the very moments I wanted to spend with them.

What began as a sidestep into consulting quickly grew into something bigger. As the business demand outpaced the work–life balance I was trying to preserve, I began hiring other working moms who had stepped away from the traditional workforce. These women were smart, driven, and deeply talented, but many had been quietly resigned to make what felt like a binary choice: stay in a system that made it nearly impossible to thrive at both work and home, or leave entirely. They didn't choose to leave because they lacked drive or talent, but because the system failed to support their realities.

Together, we built something different. My promise to them was simple: Sometimes you will have more work, which means you will have added income. Sometimes you will have more time, which means you will have extra time with your family. Both were equally valued. We shared in the risk and the reward. Year after year, we doubled our revenue until we sold the company to the largest media brand in our industry.

Along the way, I had the privilege of coaching dozens of women into careers that finally aligned with their lives. That journey taught me how powerful it can be to pause and ask a few key questions.

I invite you to consider them now:

- When you look back at your career so far, when did you feel most fulfilled?
- Describe a project, role, or experience when you felt most passionate about your work. What were you doing?
- What kind of work–life integration are you truly looking for?
- How much do you need to earn, and how much time are you willing to dedicate to work to make that possible?

(I know, I know. Everyone wishes they could be a millionaire and work just an hour a week, but let's assume a little bit of realism here.)

Step into Your Era of Intentional Selfhood (Just for a Bit)

Now, let's take this one step further. For this next activity, I want to invite you to do something you may not often do: Create your own version of Gen Z's "NarcisStory." Let the world revolve around *you* for a few minutes. This isn't to become self-centered. It's to become self-aware.

This activity assumes you're in a knowledge-based role that allows for at least some flexibility in where or when you work. I'll also acknowledge briefly that it is a wild privilege to be able to consider these options. Some may have situational or economic hardships that mean these options are not feasible. But if you're able to do so, let's dive in.

Activity: Design a Workweek That Doesn't Suck

There is no perfect schedule. But there is a better one designed by you, for you. Use this exercise to spark reflection and begin defining what works best for you.

Take time to reflect and answer the questions below. You may want to revisit them over the next few weeks, months, or even years. Experiment and take notes as you see patterns emerge. I've included notes about my learned preferences in italics for reference.

- When is it easiest for you to do focused work? Are you an early bird, a night owl, or somewhere in between?
  I love to work at 4 a.m., that's when my brain works best! (I know, not normal.)
- Where do you feel most productive for heads-down work? Is it in a quiet home office, a bustling café, or somewhere else entirely? Does it depend on the task? (For example, when writing, you like X, but for other work, you like Y.) What spaces are available to you?
  I have learned that I love to write in a bustling café. But for complex data analysis or synthesis of trends, I work best in the quiet of my home office with binaural beats playing in my earbuds. On heavy call days, I definitely need more privacy and quiet spaces.

- What personal rhythms do you need to work around? For example, if morning workouts are nonnegotiable for you, mornings may not be the best time to schedule heads-down work.
  I also get my best workouts in early, so I have learned to structure my week so that I work out every other day and the days in between are dedicated to early-morning "work shifts."
- If you live with family: What family moments matter most to you? Are you someone who wants to be home when the kids get off the bus? Or are mornings the time you most want to be present with your loved ones?
  To me, one of the most important moments of connection is getting my kids off the bus and hearing them debrief about their day. So, I am happy to adjust my focus work times to allow me to meet the daily meet up needs of my coworkers and clients, but also get my kids on and off the bus on the days I work from home.
- Do you like to travel? If so, how often? What frequency feels energizing instead of draining?
  I love to travel for work. My ideal (as I learned through trial and error) is every other week for 1–2 nights. I can't always adhere to that schedule. As a frequent keynote speaker, I go when and where the work demands. But whenever I can align with that rhythm, I do.
- What consistently makes you less productive? Is it noise, interruptions, too many meetings?
  I love talking to other people! But scheduling too many meetings is something I have to monitor closely—especially if there are too many meetings that "could have been an email."
- Do you need to see people in person every day?
  I do not. Even though I'm an extrovert, I have built a stronger relationship with my current team than any team I have worked with in a physical office. However, my husband (an introvert) absolutely loathes the work-from-home life. He MUST (literally, MUST) be in an office as much as possible for his own mental health.

Now, go back and review your answers. Star your top three work preferences, the ones that you learned matter most to you. Is there one that feels nonnegotiable? Something that, if honored, would make everything else feel more manageable?

Congratulations! You just designed your ideal workweek. Great job!

Now, let's get real: You're not going to be able to get *everything* you want. But that's not the point. The point is identifying those preferences and gaining clarity about what you value most.

Use What You've Learned to Make Smarter Trade-Offs

Maybe you've realized your job doesn't fully meet your needs, but you dread addressing these concerns with your higher-ups. It might feel like you're bracing for a negotiation: a perceived trade-off where one side loses and the other side gains. But the truth is, everyone wants to work smarter, not harder, and that includes your employer. Leaders should want to create environments that support high performance, creativity, and retention. But they can't do that effectively if they are designing in the dark.

When I am not writing books like this one, my main job is researching the world of design. I work with the interior designers, architects, workplace strategists, and product development teams that are tasked with shaping some of the most important and influential work environments in the world.

And this is what these firms are struggling with today: How can we create workspaces that truly support people if we do not understand what those people actually need? How can we design for "better" when no one has taken the time to define what "better" looks like? That is where *your* self-awareness becomes *their* greatest asset.

If work is no longer just a place we go, but an extension of our identity, then redefining what it means to *thrive* starts by grounding ourselves in what actually supports people—not in theory, but in practice.

Lead with Dialogue, Not Demands

Getting clear on what you need is powerful—but the next step is learning how to share that clarity in a way that builds trust, not tension.

The goal isn't to storm into your manager's office with a list of demands; it's to start a dialogue rooted in mutual benefit.

Begin small. Start with language that invites partnership:

- "I've been reflecting on when and where I do my best work, and I'd love to explore how that could make me even more effective on our team."
- "Here's what I've noticed helps me focus most. Can we test a version of that for a few weeks and see what happens?"

This isn't about getting everything you want—it's about finding the overlap between what fuels you and what serves the organization. Treat it like an experiment: pilot, gather feedback, adjust. The individuals that thrive will be those who can find ways to connect their needs to a mutual business benefit. The companies that thrive will be those who embrace data, empathy, and curiosity in response.

Remember: Clarity Is Kind

Even if you don't get everything you wrote down today (which would be highly unlikely!), simply knowing your non-negotiables and preferences helps you work more efficiently within the boundaries you have now. More importantly, this new level of clarity allows you to express your needs effectively—and that changes everything.

When people know what they need to do their best work, leaders can stop guessing. They can make smarter, more targeted decisions on crucial issues: how to structure teams, when to offer flexibility, what kinds of tools actually improve productivity, and where to invest in real support instead of providing surface-level perks. It shifts the focus from trying to please everyone to designing environments where the *right* conditions exist for people to thrive.

So, yes—this exercise was for *you*. But the ripple effects? They're for everyone. Because clarity is not just kind. It's contagious. And it's the foundation for a future of work that actually works.

So What? Key Takeaways from Chapter 3

- **Gen Zers are not just pushing for change.** They are reflecting a reality we are all living in, whether we recognize it yet or not.
- **We have all become more personalized in how we live, work, and make decisions.** That shift is not selfish. It is strategic.
- **Most people have never had the privilege to define *how* they work best.** Today, for the first time in history, we can.
- **Redefining what "better" looks like begins by understanding your own non-negotiables.** Identifying your own needs also helps you express them to others.
- **Designing a better workweek is not about getting everything you want.** It is about knowing what matters most so you can prioritize accordingly.
- **Clarity is contagious.** The more honest we are about what we need, the more we help create workplaces that actually work for us.

4

Rethinking Work: From Where It Happens to How It Happens

> **The big idea:** To keep up with the speed of change, companies must stop designing policies for the workforce they *used* to have—and start building systems for the talent they want to keep and *attract next*.

IN MID-2025, A well-established financial services firm rolled out a sweeping return-to-work mandate: "Four days a week in-office, effective immediately." The message came from a long-tenured executive team. Their rationale was simple: "Face time fuels performance and builds culture."

But on the ground, the reaction was anything but unified.

Jamal, a top-performing senior associate and single dad, felt blindsided. For the past few years, hybrid flexibility had helped him meet client deadlines and handle school drop-offs without missing a beat. "This isn't about laziness. It's about logistics," he said. "I always get the work done." Now, one of the company's best assets was looking for work elsewhere.

Just down the hall, Matt, a seasoned consultant managing international accounts, was baffled. His clients spanned multiple time zones, and none of them were based in his city. "Most of my meetings happen at odd hours, over Zoom. Now I'm commuting to sit in a nearly empty office, only to hop on video calls all day?" he said. "They don't realize how much time will now shift from productive work to commuting just to be seen."

Both employees were high performers. Both were committed. Yet neither felt seen. Why did this mandate miss the mark?

The fact is that, to those implementing the mandate, "return to work" means something different. To them, "work" is a *noun*, representing a fixed location where a job gets done. For Jamal and Matt, however, "work" has shifted into a *verb*. And that subtle shift in perspective transforms how many employees define productivity and manage their time—and what they expect from physical space.

This is *why the old systems don't work anymore*—because we're operating in a different grammar of work. As knowledge work becomes less about place and more about impact, leaders must adapt, or they risk not only designing for the wrong era, but also their best talent moving on.

The Real Problem: RTO Fixes the *Where*—But Not the *How*

The financial firm's return to office (RTO) mandate came from a place of good intent—but also from mistaken assumptions. It reflected what the CEO valued most, based on his own lived experiences: routine, visibility, and in-person connection. In other words, the Golden Rule in action: Treat others the way you want to be treated. But in a workforce of professionals shaped by different life stages, backgrounds, and needs, the Golden Rule often falls short.

Here's why: Most RTO mandates attempt to fix a *how* problem with a *where* solution.

ThinkLab research has identified that one of the challenges leaders struggle with the most is figuring out how to build culture within an increasingly hybrid workforce. The mistake is assuming that bringing knowledge workers back to a physical office will solve that challenge.

In our discussions with Gen Zers—and in many anecdotal stories from both our industry and others—we have heard frustrations like those voiced in the opening of this chapter. One Gen Zer even told us, "It's like my dad saying, 'Because I said so,' even when it makes no sense. If they are going to treat us like children, people are going to behave like children."

If your team struggles with remote communication, collaboration, or decision-making, bringing them back to the office won't solve it. You'll just relocate the dysfunction.

After all, communication breakdowns, decision bottlenecks, and unclear roles aren't remote-work problems—they're workflow problems. And without addressing those problems directly, bringing people together physically only creates the *illusion* of cohesion.

But creating a digital-first approach to work—one that your team can execute whether in the office full-time, working from a client site, or collaborating with an office in another time zone—is the key to cracking this code.

The Digital-First Approach for Better Work Experiences

The physical office still matters, but it's not the *only* engine of productivity anymore. Which brings us back to the bigger truth: The future of work isn't only about space—it's also about how systems *and* space work together. Lasting success depends on tight alignment between people, process, and place—in that order. The challenge today is that many are being forced to make expensive decisions about the future of *place* before the *people* and *process* pieces can culturally work themselves out.

Podcast Spotlight: "The Future of Work: An Entanglement of IT, HR, and Design"

As this episode of ThinkLab's *Design Nerds Anonymous* podcast shares, the future of work isn't about silos. It's about aligning goals at the top and making sure they flow through to the actions of each team. As episode guest and workplace expert Brett Hautop put it: "You can't just move people into new spaces and expect different results. You have to change the behaviors, too."[1]

(continued)

(*continued*)

In this episode, we explore how to change behavior in your organization, in conversation with HR expert Holly May and IT expert Bryan Hope. Here's their advice:

- **People:** Design for your actual workforce, not from leaders' assumptions.
- **Process:** Focus on clarity, collaboration, and outcomes. This will help you identify tech tools and how they can bring people together.
- **Place:** Treat the office as one tool—not the solution.

For more insights on how to integrate people, technology, and space, listen to the DNA podcast episode: "The Future of Work: An Entanglement of IT, HR, and Design."

First, Focus on People

Let's return to the game we started in Chapter 1, only this time, we'll flip the perspective from employee to employer.

As an employer, would you rather:

(a) build the future of your company with only the people you have today—with the same strengths, same blind spots, no fresh thinking?

(b) welcome an entirely new team every year, bringing in a constant surge of energy and ideas, but stuck in a never-ending cycle of onboarding purgatory?

Most leaders we ask say, "Honestly? Neither." But in our research, when forced to choose, leaders tend to opt for (b) fresh perspectives and new energy and ideas. They recognize that the future demands new thinking, even if the process of getting there feels uncertain and uncomfortable.

The truth is, if we want to recruit and lead for what is coming next, we cannot rely on outdated models. We must move forward. Because whether we are ready or not, change is already under way.

Prepare Now for the Next Generation of Leaders

We are now in the midst of a once-in-a-generation shift in the American workforce. More than 4.1 million Americans will reach the traditional retirement age of 65 each year between 2024 and 2027; this period, known as the "Peak 65" era, represents the largest surge of retirement-age individuals in U.S. history.[2] By 2030, all Baby Boomers will be 65 or older.[3]

This shift will further intensify the pressure on leadership pipelines, organizational knowledge, and workforce continuity. Generation X, the next cohort in line, is the smallest in the workforce and cannot fill the gap alone. That means millennials and even Gen Zers will need to step into leadership roles far earlier than previous generations did, often without the preparation or runway their predecessors had, and amid this awkward transition from traditional work norms to hybrid work. So, how do we ensure we are not only recruiting the next generation of top talent so necessary for our businesses to thrive, but also developing them? Too often organizations overinvest in attracting candidates while underinvesting in the systems, mentorship, and development programs that turn new hires into future leaders. The companies that thrive will be those that do both.

Shift Your Leadership Style to Match the Moment

Each generation defines for itself what it means to lead and what kind of leader it wants to follow. As younger generations move into leadership roles earlier than expected, they are not just inheriting titles. They are reshaping the very definition of leadership itself.

According to generational researchers at McCrindle, expectations have evolved[4]:

- Baby Boomers tend to value leadership that **directs**.
- Generation X looks for leaders who **coordinate**.
- Millennials prefer leaders who **guide**.
- Gen Z expects leadership that **empowers**.
- Gen Alpha expects leadership that **inspires**.

For more insights on generational shifts, listen to the DNA podcast episode, "How Will Gen Alpha Shape the World We Haven't Built Yet?" with the world's foremost generational expert, Mark McCrindle.

Naturally, the perception and practice of leadership will move away from command, control, and coordination, and toward empowerment, inspiration, and engagement. If we are not ready for this transition, we are not ready for what comes next. Companies that restructure their recruiting and upskilling efforts with these values in mind now will be far better positioned to attract and grow the next generation of managers and leaders.

Breakout Reflection: A Leadership Reframe

Where the previous chapter guided individuals, this chapter guides the organization. Look at your company through an executive lens: What if your organization's leadership model wasn't built around the people who have been here the longest—but the ones who have just arrived?

Consider:

- What assumptions about "good leadership" might no longer serve your organization's next chapter?
- When was the last time a junior team member changed your mind about something important?
- Do your current systems reward presence, or do they reward impact? Do they reward bold moves or quiet compliance?
- Are you intentional about how the work gets done? Do you encourage your teams to be intentional?
- Are expectations for communication clear?

This kind of reframing does not mean substituting one generation's values with another's. It is about designing leadership mindsets and processes that evolve with the workforce they serve.

Second, Focus on Process

As we've seen, in today's working world, *where* and *when* people work may vary, but *how* they work together is what truly drives results.

Looking ahead, some organizations will go all-in on remote work, where autonomy becomes a strategic advantage. Others will return to fully in-person models betting on proximity to build culture as their strategic advantage. But the majority of companies will exist somewhere in between. In any of these approaches *how* the work happens will be the backbone of a high-performing, flexible, and future-ready organization.

But who is best positioned to redesign these processes? A traditional approach treats policy as a top-down exercise. It used to be the case that trust was granted to authority figures, and decisions about structure flowed from the top. But that model is cracking under the pressures of modern knowledge work.

In fact, I want to suggest that building trust is shifting from a top-down to a bottom-up process. Traditional top-down sources such as mainstream news, conventional advertising, and public institutions are less trusted among younger generations. In one recent example, a study found that 72 percent of Gen Z respondents use social media and the internet for financial advice, compared with just 38 percent of

Gen X respondents.[5] This trust gap naturally translates to management in workplaces, too. In fact, according to Gallup, only 21 percent of U.S. employees strongly agree that they trust in their company's leaders.[6]

Better Tools for Translating Culture into Practice

Creating better processes starts by empowering the people tasked with carrying it out: mid-level managers. In fact, they're not just enforcing policy—they're translating it. And their biggest challenge isn't whether to offer flexibility—it's how to offer it without losing alignment.

In Chapter 10, we'll go deeper into the practical tools and structures that empower mid-level managers to translate culture into everyday action—without becoming the bottleneck or the enforcer.

Because, when teams are trusted to define *how* they work best— and held accountable to shared outcomes, not uniform behavior— companies don't lose control. They gain credibility. And in a future where culture is measured by how well people feel seen, supported, and set up to succeed, credibility is the new currency.

Podcast Spotlight: "Redefining Office Culture"

Today's best organizations aren't issuing mandates—they're building ecosystems. In this episode of ThinkLab's *Design Nerds Anonymous* podcast, the authors of the book *How the Future Works* share more details about team-level agreements and other tangible tools; how the best organizations aren't issuing mandates—they're building ecosystems. They share how to:

- Replace one-size-fits-all policies with principles and guardrails
- Empower managers to create team-level clarity
- Redesign the office for what it does best: connection, collaboration, and community

Episode guest Brian Elliott, urged: "Stop saying 'hybrid.' What we really need is a level playing field—where connection, culture, and clarity don't depend on proximity."[7]

Gain even more tangible tools for building culture by listening to this DNA podcast episode with authors Brian Elliott and Sheela Subramanian.

Make Communication Intentional: Establish a Hierarchy

Successful collaboration depends on successful communication. But in flexible environments, tool sprawl and blurred expectations can lead to constant pings, misaligned priorities, and growing frustration. Without an agreement on which channel to use for which type of message, things can get lost in translation. Even with the best of intentions, communication can falter if people don't know where to talk about what.

That's why companies need a shared system for how information flows. It doesn't need to be fancy. Just consistent.

Figure 4.1 shows one we've used at ThinkLab.

This kind of system reduces stress, restores focus, and helps people reclaim their attention.

Build the Scaffolding: Your Company-Level Non-Negotiables

If trust is being rebuilt from the bottom-up, then clarity must come from the top-down, because without it, there's no way to align count-less individual needs into a clear path forward.

But not in the form of rigid mandates or inflexible policies. What modern organizations need is a strong scaffolding—a structure that doesn't replace autonomy but *supports* it. This is where company-level non-negotiables come in.

Non-negotiables are not designed to control how people work. They are the few shared standards that help everyone understand

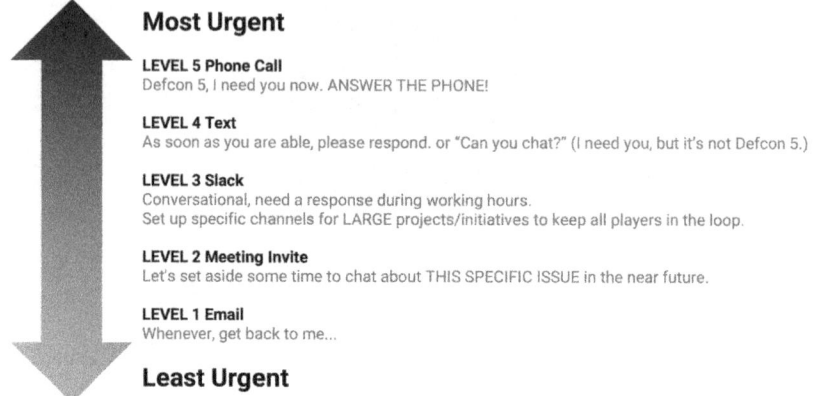

THINKLAB COMMUNICATION HIERARCHY

Most Urgent

LEVEL 5 Phone Call
Defcon 5, I need you now. ANSWER THE PHONE!

LEVEL 4 Text
As soon as you are able, please respond. or "Can you chat?" (I need you, but it's not Defcon 5.)

LEVEL 3 Slack
Conversational, need a response during working hours.
Set up specific channels for LARGE projects/initiatives to keep all players in the loop.

LEVEL 2 Meeting Invite
Let's set aside some time to chat about THIS SPECIFIC ISSUE in the near future.

LEVEL 1 Email
Whenever, get back to me...

Least Urgent

Figure 4.1   Example communication hierarchy: A simple tool teams can use to establish clear norms for when and how to communicate across channels.

Source: ThinkLab.design / with permission of ThinkLab.

what's expected of them—no matter their role, location, or team. Think of them as the behavioral backbone of your culture: not what you believe, but how you behave.

And here's the most important thing: You probably won't get them right on the first try. That's not a reason to wait—it's a reason to start. So, go ahead and draft them. Test them. Evolve them. The value lies in committing to clarity, not perfection.

To be effective, company-level non-negotiables should be:

- **Few in number.** Stick to choosing three to five. If everything is a priority, nothing is.
- **Visible.** Post them where people will actually see them—in your onboarding and on the wall (meaning both your digital "bulletin board" and physical ones).
- **Actionable.** Tie them to real behaviors, not just abstract values.

For example, if your company values responsiveness, your non-negotiable might clarify response-time expectations for external clients. If focus and collaboration are both crucial, you might define when real-time meetings should happen—and when they shouldn't. These standards give people something to align around. They don't solve every edge case, but they remove the ambiguity that so often slows teams down.

When you put it all together—the team agreements, the communication hierarchy, the non-negotiables—you create a culture that knows how to flex without falling apart. A culture where autonomy and alignment can coexist. And where everyone has just enough scaffolding to stand tall and move fast.

Finally, Focus on Place

To be successful, remote knowledge work demands that employees collaborate with intention. But even fully in-office teams must now navigate distributed tools, global time zones, and hybrid client relationships. This reality means that the office must transform to handle this new set of needs.

What Interior Design Fees Can Tell Us About the Future of the Office

At ThinkLab, we sit at the intersection of data and design. We're the team behind the nerdy number crunching that powers the *Interior Design* Giants of Design list. (Think of it like the Fortune 500, but for interiors firms.) This research gives us an inside look at the latest developments in office design.

And here's what we've seen: Between 2019 (pre-pandemic) and early 2025, overall fees for corporate sector design work dropped by 18 percent.[8] That means companies aren't just talking about change—they're voting with their dollars. But don't mistake "less volume" for "less value." A common term from the real estate world is the more apt description: "flight to quality." Those who are moving, upgrading, and rethinking their workplaces are demanding more and better than ever before.

What we're seeing isn't the death of the office—it's the elevation of it. With fewer spaces being built, there's more pressure on every square foot to perform. The physical office must now serve as a strategic tool—a place that earns the commute by offering something people can't get at home: deep connection, spontaneous collaboration, shared energy. It's what many people miss about the interior design profession: at its best, design doesn't just look good—it actively shapes behavior and enables better outcomes.

Leading Companies Are Adopting an ROI Mindset on RTO

But—as we saw in the stories that opened this chapter—forcing talent into the room doesn't guarantee alignment. After all, you can mandate presence, but you can't mandate mindset. Unless your systems and workflows are strong, you'll still struggle—just under fluorescent lights.

ThinkLab research with leading decision-makers for corporate environments reveals they are taking a different approach to return to office (RTO). The most forward-thinking companies are evaluating workplace decisions less through simple, broad policies, and more through the lens of return on investment (ROI)—determining which particular teams need to be in the office, how often, and how that presence can drive meaningful returns.

As one anonymous corporate client told us: "We gave them everything they asked for; they still aren't coming in. Now, we're moving from broad encouragement to selective enforcement. It's much more about which groups drive ROI and what those groups need from physical space."

Podcast Spotlight: "Why Traditional Workplace Metrics Are Obsolete"

In this episode of the *Design Nerds Anonymous* podcast, Rob Sadow, founder of Flex Index, a new platform that measures success for remote and in-office work policies, shares how the best organizations are rethinking their measures of success, moving from metrics focused on real-estate investment to human productivity metrics. Here are a few key takeaways:

- Traditional workplace metrics like "people per square foot" are no longer relevant in today's hybrid work environment.
- Data is driving decision-making in workplace design, from flexible work policies to daily and peak attendance patterns.
- Today, output-based metrics (such as productivity and employee engagement) are more effective than input-based metrics (such as physical presence).

Sadow shares, "The fundamental, simplest question being asked now is: What's the return on investment of an office?" He added: "That wasn't a question we asked five or ten years ago. We just took it for granted that everyone worked in the office. But now, everything from policy to space allocation to employee outcomes is under scrutiny and the old metrics can't keep up."[9]

Explore more on new metrics for measuring workplace success by listening to this DNA podcast episode with Rob Sadow.

As the Demand for Offices Declines, New Opportunities Emerge

Here's where the return-to-office conversation falls short. In our eagerness to "go back" to the ways things were, we miss overlooking what's *emerging*. The future of work isn't binary—we're not forced to make a choice between home *or* the office.

In fact, while there is indeed abundant opportunity to reimagine traditional workplaces for the better, there's also untapped potential in the spaces in-between. Coworking hubs, hospitality-driven lobbies, coffee shops, social clubs, and branded third spaces—these aren't temporary fixes. They're *growth markets*. Even as traditional corporate work slows, new possibilities are taking shape. And for the architecture and design industry, that's good news.

It's also great news for knowledge workers looking for effective workspaces outside of home and the office. And it could mean greater opportunity for companies trying to balance investments and manage risk in their own real estate portfolio.

The companies that pay attention to these latest developments won't just design better spaces. They'll design better experiences— experiences that help people do their best work, no matter where they sit.

Podcast Spotlight: "Corporate Collaboration in the Phygital Landscape"

In this episode of the *Design Nerds Anonymous* podcast, Microsoft's Matthew Marzynski and future of work expert Phil Kirschner share modern insights for future-proofing your organization, including:

- **Equity in hybrid work starts with design details.** Camera angles, audio quality, and room layouts can either bring participants together or make them feel invisible. Marzynski notes: "People aren't just exhausted by the work. They're exhausted by the friction."[10]
- **Emotional design matters as much as physical and digital design.** Kirschner shares, "The future workplace isn't just about space or tech. It's about how it *feels* to work for your company—whether people are in the office or not."
- **The office must earn the commute.** New ROI will come from giving any physical space investment a clear purpose and holding that investment accountable to deliver on that promise.

Learn more about evolving mindsets around the workplace by tuning in to this podcast episode with Microsoft's Matthew Marzynski and future of work expert Phil Kirschner.

Shift from the Golden Rule to the Platinum Rule

The Golden Rule—"Treat others the way *you* want to be treated"— has guided workplace norms for generations. But in a world where teams span time zones, life stages, and work styles, it is often inadequate. The future of work demands the *Platinum Rule*: Treat others the way *they* want to be treated.

While many of these technologies, including AI-powered workplace tools, are still in development, they're pointing us to a better future. A future where systems can reduce friction, not add to it— helping employees navigate complexity, connect with purpose, and contribute in ways that align with both business goals and personal needs.

For companies willing to make the mindset shift now, the payoff won't just be in retention or productivity—it will be in resilience. Because the best workplaces of tomorrow won't be the ones that resist change. They'll be the ones that *design for it*.

So What? Key Takeaways from Chapter 4

- **Return-to-office mandates often mistake a *location* problem for a *workflow* problem.** If the "how" is broken, changing the "where" won't fix it—you'll just relocate the dysfunction.
- **Work has become a verb, not a place.** Today's teams need clarity around *how* work gets done, not just where people sit. The most effective workplaces are intentionally designed to drive that behavior.
- **Managers are not just enforcers—they are translators.** We must empower managers to localize the broader strategy and build meaningful working rhythms rooted in trust and collaboration.
- **Communication needs a hierarchy.** Without clear expectations for *what* gets shared *where*, teams fall into tool sprawl, missed signals, and decision fatigue.
- **Clarity is the antidote to chaos in flexible work environments.** Company-level non-negotiables offer shared guardrails that make flexibility sustainable—and reduce ambiguity for everyone.
- **Establishing trust is no longer a top-down process. It's built from the bottom-up.** Leadership models, workflows, and cultural norms must reflect this shift—especially as a new generation redefines what it means to lead and follow.

5

The Future Is Speaking—But Are We Listening?

The big idea: In a world moving faster than ever, your biggest competitive advantage is fresh perspective. Innovation doesn't come from echo chambers. It comes from building systems that surface unseen ideas—and leaders bold enough to hear them.

THE FIRST PHASE of ThinkLab's generational research started with more than 15 hours of deep discussions with senior firm leaders—principals, partners, and executives across the interior design industry. They were candid, engaged, and deeply invested in the success of their teams.

We asked these firm leaders a single question: "What's the biggest challenge you're facing right now?" They were quick to answer, and nearly every conversation in our hours of candid dialogue circled back to one central theme: how to readjust analog workflows to the realities of hybrid work.

Some leaders worried about how to nurture a strong, cohesive culture in a hybrid environment. Many shared a growing concern that, without as much in-person face time, younger designers weren't getting the mentorship they needed to grow. And others simply missed the creative spark that came from being in the same room. As one leader summed it up: "I just don't know how to recreate 'the hang'—those casual moments around the coffee station that once happened so naturally."

A few weeks later, we gathered together a series of formal group discussions with emerging designers we saw as representing the future of the industry. We asked them to help us brainstorm how we might solve some of the business challenges currently faced by our firms, our industry, and, frankly, knowledge work as a whole.

Many of these discussions revolved around senior leaders' concerns about how to adapt analog workflows to fit with hybrid ways of working. But, unlike the earlier discussions with leaders, some of the younger designers spoke with a tentative energy. Finally, in one session, there was a long, awkward pause. One young designer unmuted her computer's microphone and asked, "Permission to speak freely?"

"Absolutely," I said.

"I'm sick of people talking about how hybrid is hard," she told us. "It's not hard. It's just how we work. This is really a change management issue—for older generations."

Just like that, the conversation flipped. Because to her—and to many of her peers—hybrid wasn't a challenge. It wasn't something to be solved or "figured out." It was the default, the expectation. The designer wasn't saying this out of defiance—she was just explaining her experience with unfiltered candor.

That moment reframed everything for me because it revealed just how different her perspective was. And how much we'd been missing.

We realized that, sometimes, the insight that can spark your next breakthrough isn't spoken by the loudest or most senior voice in the room. It can come from a quiet, inconspicuous voice you haven't heard—*yet*.

The Missing Link for Making Meaningful Change

Information alone won't prepare us for the future. It's about letting what you hear challenge your assumptions, expand your understanding, maybe even change your mind.

In this chapter, we'll look at how companies like Gucci, Deloitte, and even our own team at ThinkLab are bringing new voices to the table—and acting on what they learn.

What we heard in that moment with the group of Gen Z designers revealed a rift deeper than just a generational divide. It exposed a blind spot. The group of senior leaders was searching for ideas to tackle hybrid work, but the real issue wasn't a lack of ideas. It was a lack of systems to capture and act on them, especially when they didn't align with the traditional unwritten work norms.

After all, if the same voices keep weighing in, you'll keep getting the same results. But in many organizations, the voices with the freshest perspectives are the furthest from strategic decision-making. And even when they're invited in, there's rarely a system in place to make their contributions matter.

If we want to hear them, we need more than open minds. We need intentional structures that uncover the ideas we can't see on our own and make space for perspectives that challenge the status quo.

Leverage Shadow Boards to Turn Input into Action

One of the most effective models I've seen when it comes to structuring next-gen feedback is often called a shadow board. Gucci has one of the most inspiring examples. The luxury company recognized that its sales were declining as its core demographic was aging.[1] Its leaders knew doing things the same way was not going to produce different results. They recognized the need for fresh thinking and put in place a shadow board made up of employees that mirrored the younger demographic they needed to target. This board's role was to advise senior leadership on product development and marketing strategies to help the brand connect with an emerging group of consumers.

This move wasn't about replacing the old guard with the new. It was about expanding the conversation. The goal was to find new inspiration by listening to fresh perspectives that saw the world differently. One executive even described the shadow board as "a wake-up call for the executives." Importantly, leadership stayed in control. The members of the shadow board did not make decisions; they offered perspective. Leadership retained full authority to take what resonated and leave what didn't. Leaders used their experience to filter those ideas and choose which to experiment with.

The results speak for themselves. During a time when sales for one of its closest competitors declined by 11.5 percent, Gucci's surged by 136 percent. Its leaders' willingness to listen to new voices, and more importantly to act on new insights, sparked not just a revenue win but a brand transformation.

Creating a shadow board is not only about collecting new ideas—it's also about building trust. For emerging voices, especially Gen Zers, to speak honestly, they need to see that their input is taken seriously and has the potential to drive real change, or they simply stop speaking up. In our research at ThinkLab, we hear a recurring theme from Gen Zers: "I trust you when I feel trusted." For them, trust isn't built through titles or hierarchies. It's earned when leaders take action.

This does not mean that every idea shared must be used. But when leaders acknowledge contributions and make decisions transparently—explaining why certain ideas are chosen and others are not—they create a feedback loop that builds credibility and engagement. This actually begins not only to have a positive impact on the business but also to grow the next generation of talent. For this generation, psychological safety is not just about having a voice. It is about seeing that their voices make a difference.

Gucci's shadow board is an excellent example of leveraging next-gen views for marketing and product development strategies. But the possibilities of leveraging this structure to help us see into the future are nearly endless.

Adapt the Model to Fit Your Industry

As the founder of ThinkLab, I spotted an opportunity to adapt the shadow board concept to meet the specific needs of our field. ThinkLab helps product brands in categories such as furniture, flooring, lighting, and more leverage research to understand how interior designers recommend and specify products and, more importantly, how to gain their preference. And that influence is significant. The average designer has 40 times the recommendation (buying) power of the average American consumer. For designers working at the Interior Design Giants of Design, that number jumps to 140 times.[2]

But in an industry centered on the tactile experience of trying out chairs or feeling beautiful fabrics, we have struggled to adjust to the digital-first lens of younger generations. That shift is already reshaping our deeply analog approach to selling.

ThinkLab statistics indicate that while the average rep in our industry is 49, the average age of the designer initially selecting fabrics and finishes is under 26 years old. And while Gen Zers represent 18 percent of the general U.S. workforce, we estimate fewer than 7 percent of sales reps in our industry fall into this age group and generational perspective.

In 2025, ThinkLab launched our own version of a shadow board that fit our industry's unique challenges. What we call the Gen Z Cohort was created with a specific mission: to tackle the growing disconnect between an aging salesforce and a rising group of younger designers who, because of workforce gaps, are stepping into responsibility earlier—often making the first picks of fabrics and finishes before presenting options to more senior design directors.

This group of emerging designers—nominated by their firms, the American Society of Interior Designers (ASID), and *Interior Design's* "30 under 30" program—represents designers in the Gen Z and young millennial category ranging from "still a student" to 30 years old. They advise ThinkLab and the brands we serve on how to better connect with the next generation of product selectors. Simply put: We built an intentional structure for collecting insights and invited our core constituents to the table. And newsflash: As shared in our opening story around hybrid work, they often think quite differently than the established norms of this industry.

Each quarter, we gather key questions both from our research and from our partner brands on where their marketing and sales teams are struggling to connect. We conduct in-depth qualitative focus groups with our Gen Z Cohort and translate that feedback into actionable insights—helping manufacturers better serve design firms and helping design firms better engage the next generation of talent.

We gather and share these insights in quarterly summaries, and, as with Gucci's shadow board, senior leaders filter the input and decide which ideas to act upon: for example, how to build relationships with Gen Z designers, where to find mentorship gaps, or which marketing tools and sales tactics break through the noise. Many leaders have even used these insights to evolve their own internal workflows.

There are also countless insights that our partner brands are now armed to share with design firms, many of whom are still trying to solve the hybrid workflow challenge introduced in the opening story. Here's what one participating executive had to say:

> "Our experience with ThinkLab's Gen Z Cohort has been eye-opening. It's helped us look at an industry we've been part of for decades through a completely new lens. We've gained tangible ideas for our sales teams—especially how our seasoned sellers can better connect with the next generation of designers.
>
> But what surprised us most was the internal impact. Inspired by this initiative, we're now exploring new ways to strengthen our leadership development efforts. We see real potential in creating opportunities for emerging talent to share their perspectives with managers and leaders, and we are actively considering new approaches to make that happen. It's part of a bigger shift: We know the leadership gap is real, and we're taking intentional steps to prepare for our next generation of leaders."
>
> **—Cindy Kaufman, VP of Marketing,
> Mannington Commercial**

This approach is not limited to fashion or interior design. Any company in any industry can take a similar step. You begin by being intentional about who you invite into the conversation and what you do with the insights once you actually hear what those voices are saying.

Learn from How Other Industries Are Listening Better

Shadow boards, or any structure that brings emerging voices into strategic conversations, can be applied across industries to solve many different types of challenges. (See the "Next-Gen Shadow Boards in Action" sidebar.) While Gucci offers a first-class example, and ThinkLab's approach has already been quite successful, we are far from alone in adopting shadow boards. Across industries, companies are using similar models with measurable results.

Next-Gen Shadow Boards in Action

Across industries, forward-thinking companies are tapping into the insights of younger talent through shadow boards and similar models. Here are a few standouts:

American Nurses Association
To stay relevant to a younger workforce, the ANA created a millennial and Gen Z advisory group.[3] This initiative brought younger nurses into conversations around leadership, governance, and strategy, helping modernize the association from within.

AccorHotels
After struggling to connect with millennial travelers, AccorHotels formed a shadow board of younger employees.[4] This group launched the Jo&Joe brand and developed the Accor Pass, a subscription service targeting travelers under 25 years old. Their work helped the company realign with a younger audience and respond more effectively to their needs.

Deloitte
Deloitte's Junior Advisory Board gives millennial and Gen Z employees a seat at the table for strategic discussions.[5] It fosters two-way communication and allows junior team members to contribute meaningfully to the direction of the organization.

Estée Lauder
Through a reverse mentoring program, Estée Lauder pairs senior leaders with younger employees who provide insight into digital trends and cultural shifts.[6] This cross-generational exchange has helped influence both strategy and leaders' mindsets.

Oliver Wyman
The management consulting firm created a shadow advisory board called the Global Leadership Team Council, made up of

(continued)

(*continued*)

employees below the executive or director level. This group works directly with senior leaders on company-wide initiatives, including shaping employee recognition programs and influencing company values and policies. The initiative was credited with helping reduce attrition by 30 percent in 2022.[7]

While each approach looks different, they all share one common thread: they create intentional space for emerging voices and translate listening into action.

The format may vary, but the principle stays the same. Innovation thrives when organizations are intentional about hearing perspectives that differ from the norm. How can we rethink and unlearn if we don't bring in a fresh perspective? Whether you lead a start-up or a legacy brand, whether you are in manufacturing, media, finance, or another field, the opportunity is available to those who seize it.

Activity: A Challenge for Leaders—Who Is Missing from Your Table?

The future belongs to those who can hear the voices that others disregard. Not just because it is the right thing to do, but because it is essential to staying relevant, competitive, and innovative. After all, new ideas rarely come from familiar perspectives. They emerge when someone sees a challenge through a different lens, asks a new kind of question, or spots a signal others have missed.

These new voices can open new markets, attract new talent, and help your company evolve—but only if you build structures that make space for them and prove their input matters.

If you are ready to take action, consider launching a shadow board. Here is how to get started:

1. **Define the problem you wish to solve.**
2. **Select 6 to 12 participants** who bring a range of perspectives. They can be internal employees, external advisors, or a mix of

the two, depending on the problem you want to solve. The key is to select people who understand your business well enough to provide grounded, relevant ideas but not so well that they can't remain open to breaking the mold.

3. **Think beyond titles.** Prioritize diversity of thought, background, race, gender, and generation. As the most racially and ethnically diverse generation in U.S. history, Gen Z brings cultural fluency, paired with digital-first instincts, and can help you anticipate where your industry is going next.[8]

4. **Seat the board for at least one year,** with a minimum of quarterly meetings. This gives time for trust and ideas to develop.

5. **Ensure senior leadership support.** This cannot be a side project. If you are asking for input, you must be prepared to act on it—even if it challenges your assumptions.

6. **Choose a strong facilitator.** This person should create a safe, inclusive space to encourage feedback and help turn it into insights leadership can use. In some cases, a member of the cohort can lead this role, building ownership and accountability within the group.

7. **Make sure to kick off every new meeting with a summary of ideas implemented or in the works.** This is a best practice developed in our ThinkLab shadow board that helps ensure the voices at the table stay engaged.

If you are not ready to launch a formal shadow board, you can still start small. Pause and reflect on the following:

- Who is not currently part of your decision-making process?
- What perspectives are missing?
- What business goal are you trying to reach—whether it's attracting younger talent, better serving a diverse customer base, or staying ahead of cultural shifts?
- And who might already have the answers you need, if only they were invited to the table?

Whether you are starting big or small, the goal is the same: create space for intentional listening. When people feel trusted, they trust you in return. And when they see that their input leads to action, they are more likely to bring forward the ideas that can truly move your business forward.

Start Where You Are, But Do It with Intention

Creating space for new voices is not just inclusive—it's strategic. Whether through a formal shadow board or a simple shift in how you gather input, the message is clear: The future is already speaking. The question is: Are you willing to hear it?

The conversations about how we work are shifting, and so is the way we lead. In Part III, we reveal 10 fundamental shifts emerging from our research across generations. These are not just trends. They are signals. And they offer the clearest picture yet of where work is headed and how to get ahead of it.

So What? Key Takeaways from Chapter 5

- **Listening can be transformative.** Growth comes when leaders question assumptions, lean into discomfort, and allow new voices to reshape the path forward.
- **Without structure, good ideas get lost.** Insight doesn't become action unless there's a system to capture, filter, and apply it.
- **Shadow boards are a powerful way to bring emerging voices into strategic conversations.** They allow leadership to retain decision-making authority while expanding perspective.
- **Trust is built through follow-through.** Sharing what actions were taken (or not) and why is essential to keeping next-gen contributors engaged.
- **The shadow board model works across many industries.** From Gucci to Deloitte to the American Nurses Association, forward-thinking organizations are leveraging next-gen insights to innovate.

PART

10 Fundamental Shifts

Now that we've set the stage with the foundational concepts, it's time to explore 10 key shifts that are transforming how we think about the future—shifts uncovered through ThinkLab's deep dive into Gen Z's world. (Remember that these shifts go beyond Gen Z. Our research looked at data across generations to spot the trends shaping us all.)

We expected to find a straight, predictable line pointing to "the future." Instead, what we discovered in many cases looked more like a pendulum swing—a pattern we call the **"Boomer-ang Effect"** (Figure III.1). Rather than a clean progression from one generation to the next—a predictable trend line in which, say, new ways of working were adopted in greater numbers over time—our data often showed Gen Zers' views looping back to align more closely with those of Boomers and Gen Xers rather than with Millennials.

WHAT WE EXPECT TO SEE   **WHAT WE ACTUALLY SAW**

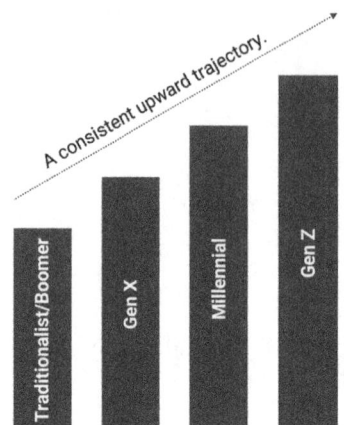
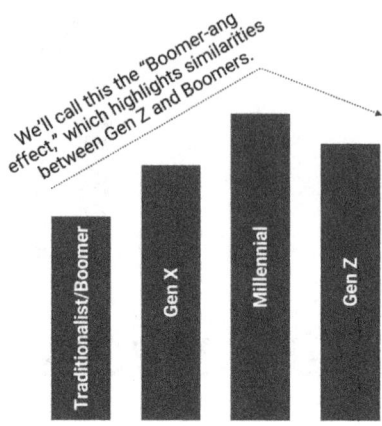

Figure III.1   The Boomer-ang Effect: We expected a clear pattern in the data—a steady increase in perception around each idea. Instead, the data often told a different story: Gen Z preferences frequently align more with Baby Boomers, but the nuance lies in how they hope those shared values come to life.

But don't be fooled: While the charts suggest these generations share certain values—like a desire for face-to-face connection and a healthy skepticism of the status quo—how they express those values in action can be quite different from one another. And that nuance is what we'll be unpacking in the next 10 chapters.

How I suggest you approach exploring our 10 fundamental shifts:

If you're a Type A, "start at the beginning and don't skip a word" kind of reader, by all means, read straight through and enjoy the journey.

But if you're more of a "wanderer," feel free to skip around. Find the shift that sparks your curiosity and start there. Each chapter is designed to stand on its own, so you can chart your own course.

Either way, I can promise this: These shifts will challenge the way you see what's ahead—and maybe even how you operate in the future.

6

Shift 1

From Physical to "Phygital": The Future Belongs to Digital Natives

> **The big idea:** In an increasingly digital world, the real competitive advantage isn't choosing between remote and in-person work—it's learning to use one to reinforce the other. Digital sparks connection; face-to-face makes it stick.

THINK BACK FOR a second. If you're over 35, what did you do when you came home from school? Chances are, you dropped your backpack, ran outside, and headed straight to the park to see who was around. Connecting with your friends started face-to-face.

Compare that with what happens when my Gen Z and Gen Alpha kids come home today. Before they ever step outside, they're already "with" their friends—group texting, hopping on Discord, or building entire worlds together in Minecraft. Sometimes, after that digital hangout, they meet up in person, but only if there's a reason to. (Kickball still holds a certain power!)

But this new pattern isn't just about childhood friendships. It's shaping how an entire generation now expects to show up at work.

Now, picture this: It's the first day of school, junior high cafeteria. You've got your tray, your lunch, and zero familiar faces. You scan the room, heart pounding, looking for somewhere safe to land. That feeling—vulnerable, exposed, on the outside looking in—is exactly how many Gen Zers describe feeling on their first day in a new office.

Other generations can, of course, recall feeling the same way at that age. But the difference for *this* generation is that up until now, they've *always* had their digital networks to lean on. Previous generations never did. So now, to walk into a physical room without those? That's a whole new challenge.

Part of what's driving this difference comes from the divide between analog natives and digital natives, according to Hannah Grady Williams, an accomplished author, TEDx speaker, and Gen Z advisor to CEOs.[1] As Williams explains, if you're over 35, you were raised as an "analog native," so your instinct is to think analog first, digital second. If you're under 30, you're likely a "digital native," wired the other way around. Yes, you can learn to "immigrate" to the other mindset, just as you can move countries—but it never fully changes where you started.

Podcast Spotlight: "Fostering Authentic Relationships with Gen Z"

In this episode of the *Design Nerds Anonymous* podcast, ThinkLab hosts author Hannah Grady Williams to explore how the rise of native digitals—those under 30 who see the world through a digital lens first—has huge implications for how we build connection at work.

Here are some key insights from our conversation:

- **Rethink what it means to connect human to human.** Every generation craves connection, but they create it differently. When analog natives apply their logic to digital natives, it can backfire. What feels human to one generation can feel like a barrier to another.
- **Invite co-creation.** Ask younger employees, "If you were in my role, what would you do differently?" Listening creates trust and unlocks fresh ideas.

- **Make face-to-face time meaningful.** For Gen Zers, honoring their digital-first fluency while also creating meaningful moments offline is key. For Gen Z, digital is default; live interactions stand out when used for recognition, mentoring, or feedback.

As Williams, puts it: "Digital is the air we breathe. For native digitals, face-to-face isn't the norm—it's the exception. That's why when it happens, it has to be intentional and meaningful."[2]

For more tips about how the rise of native digitals can strengthen how we build connection at work, listen to this DNA podcast episode with Hannah Grady Williams.

ThinkLab's research uncovered something fascinating: Gen Zers don't think in terms of "digital versus real life" the way the rest of us do. In our research, they were almost completely blind to their own fluidity between the digital and the physical realms. For them, those worlds are already blended. They use digital tools to spark relationships and to make in-person time more intentional.

In fact, thriving in today's digital-first workplace requires all of us to be intentional. After all, when you work remotely, or even in a hybrid format, connection doesn't just happen by accident. As with any long-distance relationship, you have to set aside time, show up, and build connection on purpose.

But there's an unexpected twist: Despite their tech-native reputation, Gen Zers don't want to work solely through screens. In fact, data from Gallup shows Gen Zers are the *least* likely generation to want to be fully remote—and also, along with Millennials, the *least* likely to want to be in the office five days a week.[3] What they're asking for is balance, autonomy, and the opportunity to have purposeful interactions. What if, by helping them achieve that, we made it even *more likely* for Gen Z professionals to want to show up in person?

The future of connection is what we call "phygital" (physical + digital): starting relationships online, then deepening them face-to-face.

In this chapter, we'll explore why this approach doesn't work just for digital natives—it could help all of us use our most valuable resource—time—more wisely.

Side note: I'll also call your attention to the fact that I have followed my own advice from Chapter 6 by creating a "phygital" experience. As you have read, each podcast spotlight gives you an opportunity to put down the book, or step away from your screen, take a walk, and dive deeper into insights from our experts as you choose (and only on the concepts you choose).

Oh, and one more thing as you read on: "IRL" is Gen Z slang for "in real life."

The Surprising Paradox of IRL Connection in a Digital-First World

Let's start with the numbers.

According to ThinkLab research, 74 percent of respondents told us they believe they can build strong work relationships without ever meeting in real life.[4] And who feels this most strongly? Not Gen Z, as you might expect—it's actually Millennials, at 78 percent. This is one of the first places we see what we call the "Boomerang Effect," as shown in Figure 6.1. When it comes to building relationships remotely, while Millennials are once again the most extreme, data on Gen Z's attitudes start to swing back to align more closely with those of Baby Boomers and Gen X.

DO YOU BELIEVE YOU CAN BUILD
RELATIONSHIPS WITHOUT EVER MEETING
SOMEONE IN REAL LIFE?

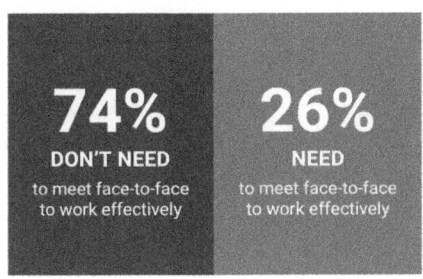

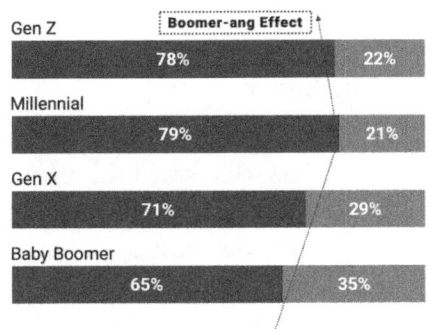

Figure 6.1   Most professionals (74 percent) say they don't need to meet in person to build relationships at work—a view led by Millennials, not Gen Z.

Source: ThinkLab.design Gen Z research / with permission of ThinkLab.

Most people believe they can work just fine without ever being in the same room. But here's where it gets really interesting. When we asked, "What's the primary way you make new professional connections?" Gen Z ranked in-person networking events and their employer's physical office higher than any other generation.

And that's a nuance that can't be explained by the data alone. Yes, many of us—including Gen Z—*can* work entirely remotely. We have the tools. But as our research discussions make clear, that doesn't mean it's how most of us actually *want* to build relationships. While Gen Z stands out for how naturally they form connections online, they're not alone in craving a chance to deepen those relationships in person.

In fact, across every generation, the data and the stories agree: Relationships still develop faster and run deeper when there's at least some face-to-face time. Digital connection is the spark; in-person connection is the fuel.

So, paradoxically, the very generation most fluent in digital life is telling us: If you want them to show up in person, first fuel that feeling of digital connection.

In Their Own Words: How Gen Z Builds Connection

These are real quotes from people gathered during our ThinkLab research:

"I start online—it's faster. But once I feel connected to someone, that's when I want to meet in person."

"I don't need a 30-minute meeting for information I can find in two minutes. Save the in-person time for conversations that matter."

"It's not that we don't value face-to-face—we do. It's just that it has to feel intentional, not forced."

How to Make Work "Phygital": Practical Ideas for Leaders and Teams

So, what do we do with this surprising insight?

If digital is the preferred starting point for Gen Z and face-to-face is the point of deeper connection, then our job as leaders, colleagues, and organizations is to build bridges between the two. It means rethinking how we welcome people, how we foster relationships, and how we use technology—not as a substitute for human interaction, but as a means to facilitate more natural and more valuable in-person moments.

Next, we'll look at five ways to put this phygital mindset into practice.

Idea #1: Build Digital On-Ramps

That "first day in the cafeteria" feeling doesn't just vanish when you grow up. Walking into a new company—especially in a hybrid world—can feel just as daunting.

One of the simplest ways to smooth that transition is to start a digital connection first, before a new hire ever sets foot in the office. Think about integrating new hires into your company via the tools they already use, as well as giving them digitally accessible ways to get to know their colleagues.

Here's how:

1. **Share short, authentic "day in the life" videos** that show what it's really like to work there.
2. **Create a simple "meet the team" document** with photos, roles, and a bit of personal background. (See Figure 6.2 for one example.)
3. **Include a photo, headshot, or link to your LinkedIn profile** or in your email signature so there's a face behind the name/email. (Believe it or not, young designers cite this as one of the single most impactful things for building new relationships with sales reps, because they can then connect the email address with a face when they meet them IRL.)

These unpolished, approachable touches make a big difference for digital natives who are accustomed to finding their bearings online before they enter a new space. And because we know from Chapter 1 that Gen Zers stay for shorter stints in a given role (we'll dive even deeper into tenure in Chapter 9!), it's not just nice for companies to empower these connections during onboarding—it's a retention strategy.

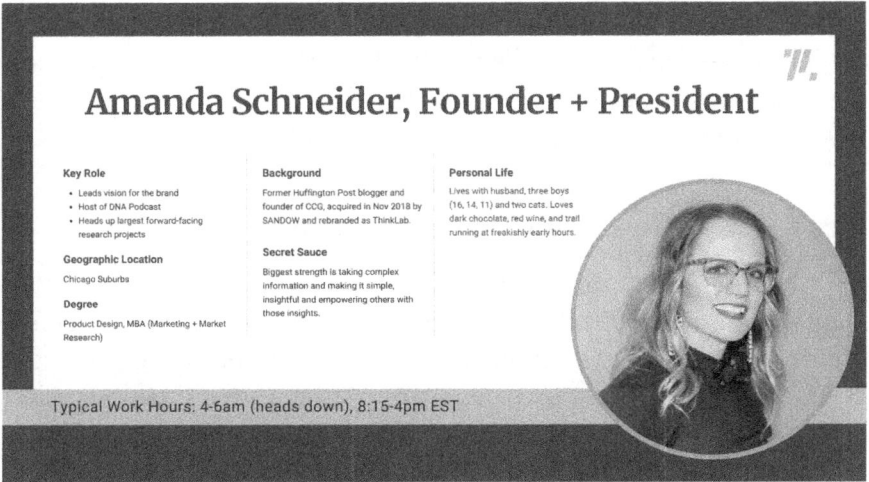

Figure 6.2   A sample page from our "meet the team" document at ThinkLab.

Idea #2: Encourage Digital Team-Building

The trick to building connection beyond the onboarding stage is to weave it into channels that feel natural and low-pressure for a generation that is used to blending online and offline life. It has to become part of the everyday rhythm of work.

Digital team-building can take many forms:

- **Shared challenges,** such as step counts or reading goals, that give colleagues easy entry points for conversation.
- **A "watercooler" channel** on Slack or Teams where people can share casual updates, such as photos from the weekend or a favorite playlist.
- **Affinity spaces** (lighthearted ones such as a "fun cats" or "fun dogs" channels, or even groups that support other ethnic or cultural identities your employees may hold) that can help employees find others with similar interests, creating micro-communities that may later translate into in-person friendships.
- **Buddy systems** that pair new or younger employees with someone just a bit more experienced. Unlike a formal mentorship program, these buddies create a "safe space" for the kinds of questions that may feel too small or awkward to ask in a regular meeting.

These seemingly small digital rituals have an outsized impact. For digital natives, sharing bits of life online first becomes a natural bridge to showing up and connecting in the real world.

Idea #3: Make In-Person Time Purposeful

In a hybrid world, the most precious commodity is time together. Digital tools are perfect for sharing information; reserve in-person moments for bonding, brainstorming, and culture-building. Don't assume people will show up to an event just because it's on their calendar. Give them a reason to come.

What this looks like:

- **Make project updates digital.** Use shared documents, Slack channels, or dashboards to track projects so live time can focus on conversation, not status reports.

- **Prioritize face time based on function.** Instead of forcing in-office time on specific days of the week, consider making specific meeting types mandatory. Example: All design charettes will be hosted in the office, usually on Tuesdays.
- **Rethink social events.** Gen Z told us loud and clear: "I drink, but many of my peers do not. We have to do better than just another happy hour to make us feel like we belong." Consider alternatives such as cooking classes, volunteering opportunities, or wellness-focused meetups.

When face-to-face time is purposeful and inclusive, people walk away energized, not drained, and are much more likely to keep showing up.

Idea #4: Develop a Culture ~~Committee~~ Community

Culture doesn't just happen by chance; it's shaped by the people who create it. And while most leadership teams have good intentions, they often overlook one of their best assets: the voices of those who naturally live and breathe a digital-first mindset.

Gen Z employees may be less experienced, but they can serve as powerful guides in designing connection that feels intuitive to their generation—and fresh to everyone else. While a culture committee meets to *discuss* ideas, a culture community connects to *act* on ideas. So, instead of a top-down "culture committee" that sets priorities, gather a cross-generational culture community to co-create experiences.

In practice:

- **Bring in fresh voices.** Put out an open call for participants, intentionally including Gen Zers (and younger Millennials) who might not usually have a seat at the table. Go back and read Chapter 5 for more ideas on how to empower these committee members. (Hint: Run with their ideas.)
- **Experiment with recreating "the hang."** Encourage casual, low-stakes ways to connect, such as virtual "office hours" across locations, informal podcast club meetups (listen in advance, then grab a brown bag lunch + discuss!), or even topic-focused casual chats. (ThinkLab hosts a chat with our sister media brands

around the use of AI that includes monthly meetups plus a dedicated Slack channel.) These are informal meetings that can be virtual or IRL and focus on a topic that upskills the individuals *and* benefits the company.

- **Make it visible.** Share photos, snippets, and outcomes from these efforts on internal channels to normalize a culture of experimentation and fun. Our parent company, SANDOW Design Group, does this through a weekly internal newsletter that regularly has a nearly 80% open rate.

This kind of digital-first approach may not feel instinctive. That's exactly why empowering the voices who *are* fluent in it can transform how culture gets built.

Idea #5: Model the Mix

Hybrid connection works best when leaders show—through their own behavior—that digital and in-person aren't competing. They're complementary. The most powerful way to influence a culture is to model it. Leaders who balance accessibility online with intentional facetime send a clear signal: It's not about choosing remote *or* in-office, it's about using both well.

How to lead by example:

- **Be present in digital spaces.** Join Slack channels, respond to chat threads, and post occasional personal updates so people see leaders as approachable, not distant.
- **Show up on purpose.** When you're in person, make that time visible: Walk the floor, join brainstorming sessions, and have informal conversations that wouldn't take place on Zoom.
- **Blend formats.** Kick off big in-person meetings with a short, asynchronous video update sent in advance, then use live time for discussion.

- **Demonstrate balance.** Share how you prioritize time away from screens (e.g., by scheduling no-meeting blocks, available-by-phone-only "office hours," or walking meetings) while still staying accessible.
- **Acknowledge the shift.** Talk openly about the value of both "sides" of hybrid: how digital tools keep work efficient and how face time deepens trust.

When leaders model this mix, it normalizes a culture that uses technology as a bridge, not a barrier—and makes "phygital" connection a daily habit across the organization.

Whether your organization's policy is five days a week in the office, fully remote, or somewhere in between, these five strategies will apply to you. After all, even if you're fully back in the office, you're now likely collaborating with other offices. And when we use digital tools intentionally to build trust and belonging with colleagues near and far, we make in-person time matter more. And in a world where connection is currency, that balance benefits every company and every generation.

The Future of Phygital

These strategies are geared toward solving today's challenges—but they're also a glimpse of where we're headed.

Each chapter in Section III explores a shift—from outdated assumptions to emerging realities. The evolution at the heart of this one is this:

FROM: Work is physical.

- It has a set time and place.
- The workday runs from 9 to 5 (roughly) and is anchored in a physical office.
- Showing up is an indicator of contribution.

TO: Work is phygital.

- Digital sparks connection; face-to-face makes it stick.
- Time and place are tools, not rules.
- The strongest teams use digital to enable access and efficiency—and in-person moments to deepen trust, culture, and belonging.

Looking Ahead: A Glimpse of 2050

If we start building cultures that balance digital connection with purposeful face-to-face time now, what might the workplace look like a generation from today? What happens when digital tools become so seamless that they don't compete with in-person connection?

Let's look ahead to a possible future in 2050: Imagine a world where your "first day" at a new company already began months earlier—inside an immersive digital community where you've already met your team, collaborated on small projects as part of the interview process, and built trust.

By the time you step into a physical office, it feels like walking into a room of old friends. Offices themselves will look different, too, with fewer rows of desks and more open spaces designed for experiences: pop-up studios, learning labs, and connection hubs that exist to do what digital can't. And because technology will make remote collaboration seamless, the choice to gather in person will be just that: a choice. A purposeful one.

So What? Key Takeaways from Chapter 6

This first shift—from physical to phygital—isn't just a Gen Z trend. It's a wake-up call for all of us about how connection happens in a digital-first world.

- **Digital first, not digital only.** Digital tools are now the starting line for relationships, but they're not the finish line. Use them to spark connection, not to replace it.
- **Intentionality wins.** In a hybrid world, connection doesn't happen by accident. Like a long-distance relationship, it takes planning, effort, and meaningful moments.
- **Connection is currency.** Whether you're in the office five days a week, fully remote, or somewhere in between, belonging and trust drive engagement and retention.
- **Going "phygital" benefits everyone.** These strategies aren't just for digital natives—they help every generation use time more wisely by letting digital handle efficiency and reserving face-to-face for what matters most.
- **Culture is a choice.** The leaders and teams who intentionally blend digital and in-person connection will build stronger cultures than those who rely only on face-to-face, in-office means.

7

Shift 2

From Authority to Authenticity: How to Build Trust in the Digital Age

> **The big idea:** In a world where everyone can see behind the curtain, trust comes from clarity, consistency, and authenticity—not perfection. Show up the same way online and in person, and you'll earn the only real competitive advantage: the trust of your employees and customers.

THERE WAS A time when projecting certainty was the key to building trust as a business. Leaders never admitted what they didn't know. They never showed any of the behind-the-scenes messiness. A polished presentation was the gold standard and signaled integrity.

But that was before everyone had a search bar in their pocket and the world literally at their fingertips. And, before change was happening as rapidly as it is today.

Now, companies are pulling back the curtain. Employees, customers, and partners know more about your organization than ever. And in this world, they aren't swayed by the perfect, polished script. The leaders who thrive now build trust together with their teams, show up the same way online and in person, and let curiosity replace polish and posturing.

We now look for signs a company is open, consistent, and easy to work with. And the habits we form as consumers—looking for transparency and simplicity—spill over into every other interaction with a company. They shape how we choose an employer, a brand, and even a business partner.

Whether you're a candidate for an interview, a customer, or a business client, the core question never changes: Can I trust you?

That trust is no longer built by what a company *says* about itself—it's built by what a company *does*. After all, people don't trust brands like Jeep or Patagonia simply because of their advertising campaigns or websites. They trust them because those brands have earned their reputations through their actions, through the behavior of real people—their employees, customers, and community members—and what those people say about them.

For example: You might buy a Jeep Wrangler because of its rugged nature featured in images and advertising. (I did!) But those images can't fully capture the quirky culture that has sprung up around driving Jeeps: Every time a Jeep Wrangler owner passes another, they give a special "Jeep wave." (Picture three fingers in the air—thumb, pointer, and middle—while gripping the steering wheel.) Also, as a Wrangler owner, if you come out of a store to find a tiny rubber duck on your car door handle, you've been "ducked." It's a tiny but significant signal that means "I see you" and "You're part of something good." While the vibe starts with the advertising, the community extends to the actual humans driving the vehicles and connects them to one another.

Similarly, customers who wear Patagonia clothing closely identify with the brand, which is committed to protecting the environment. They believe the brand's mission statement ("We're in business to save our home planet") because they've seen the company make hard decisions that back those words up. Consumers see that play out in Patagonia's policy to donate 1 percent of sales to grassroots environmental organizations to raise awareness and promote policy change. Or in its "Don't Buy This Jacket" ad against conspicuous consumption. Or in its "Worn Wear" initiative to repair used clothes. These initiatives may go against the company's bottom line, but they make the policy feel real.

That's what distinguishes brands today. They feel reliable. They feel real. They feel like a community you want to be a part of.

Choose the Company You Keep—Wisely

These high expectations don't end at the consumer level.

Today, working for a company is more than a job—it's a reflection of your own brand. When you pick a company, you're saying to the world, "This is who I'm aligned with." When you interview with a new organization, you fall down the same rabbit hole everyone does. You've looked at the company's official website, of course, but that's just marketing copy. You know to dig deeper: Glassdoor reviews, LinkedIn posts from employees, the comments on Reddit, even a personal YouTube video an employee made about their "day in the life."

Being Authentic Is More Important Than Being Perfect

After all, what matters isn't just the polish of a website. It's what shows up in the unscripted moments. Does the brand's sustainability statement translate into real action, or is it just an empty promise? Are employees encouraged to be authentic and share their views on social media, or does the company edit what they are *allowed* to say? Do brands own up to shortcomings? Even those Glassdoor reviews: Do they ring true, or do they feel manufactured? As a prospective employee, you're searching for hidden clues about whether or not the company lives out the values that the website says it stands for.

Patagonia stands out in how it treats its employees as an extension of its mission. The company offers unique benefits such as paid time off for environmental activism and environmental internships (up to two months paid for volunteering). Employees are empowered and even encouraged to act on company values—for example, choosing to attend climate rallies or influencing grantmaking decisions—which translates to pride in their employer. The proof is in the pudding: Patagonia's turnover rates are far below the national average—just 8 percent at headquarters compared to the U.S. average of 11.6 percent.[1]

The lesson is clear: Too much polish can make a company look perfectly put together, but lifeless. But a messy, transparent, encouraging message about where we have work to do—and how employees are making that happen—builds trust.

Leadership Actions Can Reinforce or Erode Trust

And here's an important nuance: The question of trust doesn't disappear the day you sign the offer. The same instincts you used to evaluate a company from the outside—"Does what I see match what they say?"—become the instincts that shape whether trust grows or erodes after you're hired.

Recent data indicates that companies are finding it harder than ever to cultivate that trust with their employees. Here's one sobering finding: According to the 2025 Edelman Trust Barometer, only 63 percent of global respondents say they trust their employer—down sharply from 77 percent in 2020. In the United States, that number is even lower.[2] As Edelman's report states: "The measurement for 'Trust in my employer' continues to decline, with less than two thirds of employees globally expressing trust in their organization's leadership."

This chapter is about that very gap—the erosion of trust in organizations and leadership—which is even more striking once we break it down by generation. A recent Wake Forest University study shows just how wide the generational trust gap has become. Over half of Gen Z and younger millennial leaders (ages 28–34) say they are dissatisfied with leadership in their industries—nearly 20 points higher than older generations. And what they want to see most in their leaders isn't authority. It's authenticity.

As Wake Forest professor Pat Sweeney explains, younger generations see leaders as "facilitators, resource providers, and coaches, rather than sources of authority."[3] They're looking for inclusion in decision-making, transparency, purpose, and an ethical culture that matches their values. In other words, they don't just want leaders who *look* in charge; they want leaders they can actually trust.

One organization that's getting this right is software company Atlassian.

At Atlassian, transparency isn't a buzzword—it's the backbone of the company's identity. One of its core values, "Open company, no bullsh*t," sets the tone from the top-down. Leadership treats information as open by default, sharing major decisions internally long before they hit the press. For example, when Atlassian decided to go public, employees knew months in advance. Sales milestones, product updates, even setbacks and losses—these aren't hidden behind closed doors; they're shared openly with the entire team in weekly all-hands town halls.

The shift to remote work put this commitment to transparency to the test. But leaders didn't pretend to have all the answers. Instead, they hosted regular video updates, acknowledged the unknowns, and empowered volunteer "champions" to share best practices across teams.

The payoff is clear: Atlassian's own research shows transparency is one of the top drivers of employee happiness.[4] By leading with honesty, openness, and a willingness to share the messy parts of growth, Atlassian has built not just a high-performing company, but one deeply trusted by its employees.

The Way We Build Trust Applies to Brands We Buy from, Too

In our personal lives, we've been trained to expect transparency. You can track a pizza to your door minute by minute. You know exactly when a rideshare will arrive. Every time a company delivers on our expectations, the trust deepens.

We now expect the same from business-to-business (B2B) relationships. But the consequences on failing to deliver far outweigh the simple inconvenience of a delayed pizza or canceled rideshare. With millions of dollars and years of partnership at risk, the stakes for B2B blind spots can be incredibly high. Every business buyer is still a consumer at heart, but the transactions are larger, the timelines longer, and the cost of a wrong decision far greater—which means the trust threshold is higher, too. Yet most B2B companies struggle to cultivate the same level of transparency and authenticity that builds trust today.

In B2B, Trust Has Gone Phygital

A recent LinkedIn post nailed it:

> Imagine if B2C companies hid information like the average B2B SaaS website: Want to know the calories in this protein bar? Talk to an "expert." Does it include peanuts? Sign up for this webinar to find out. How much does it cost? Let's set up a consultation.[5]

We laugh because we know this wouldn't work. In business-to-consumer (B2C), hiding basic information would be absurd. You simply wouldn't buy that protein bar, and you'd move on to find another snack. Yet in B2B, many organizations still operate this way—hoarding data behind gated forms or forcing potential partners into unnecessary calls. The irony is that these very tactics, once designed to generate "leads," now jeopardize trust before you even have the opportunity to meet and shake hands.

That's because the line between digital and in person connection has blurred. A negative online impression might mean never getting a chance to follow up with that person, and you may never even know it.

In a hybrid world, the companies that win are the ones that show up consistently everywhere: across both digital and physical worlds. That's what we explored in Chapter 6 when we introduced the concept of "phygital": the seamless blend of digital and in-person experiences. If you skipped that chapter, you may want to flip back—because the phygital lesson applies here, too. The more authentic and consistent a company is across every space—online, on Zoom, and across a conference table—the faster trust grows.

Podcast Spotlight: "How to Build Trust with B2B Clients in Today's Digitally Transparent Era"

As McKinsey Partner Julia McClatchy explains in this episode of *Design Nerds Anonymous*, this shift in expectations is changing how B2B clients choose partners: "B2B buyers now expect a balance: one-third in person, one-third remote, and one-third self-service. If you're not present and clear across all three, you're not even in the trust game."[6]

Throughout the episode, McClatchy shares McKinsey research about how the rules of trust in B2B business exchanges have changed. Transparency and multichannel consistency matter more than ever. In a hybrid world, people want to feel seen—not sold to.

Key insights:

- **Connection happens everywhere.** B2B buyers use an average of 10 different channels before ever talking to you—and expect seamless, consistent experiences across all of them.[7]
- **Trust grows through consistency.** Whether online, remote, or in person, the same level of openness has to show up in every interaction. Buyers want to explore and research on their own, but they also want to know a human is there to help answer questions when it counts.
- **Clarity wins.** The companies gaining share are those that reduce friction, personalize information, and show up where and how clients prefer to engage.

Listen to this DNA podcast episode to learn more from McKinsey research about how to build trust in B2B business exchanges today.

How to Build Trust in a Transparent World: Practical Ideas for Leaders and Teams

So, what can we do with all of this?

If polish and authority are no longer effective enough, then our job as leaders, colleagues, and organizations is to cultivate trust in new ways—ways that are grounded in authenticity, openness, and connection.

Let's explore three ways to start building that kind of trust from the inside out.

Idea #1: Get Clear on What You Stand for—And Live It

There's a fitting line in the musical *Hamilton* that applies here: "If you stand for nothing, what'll you fall for?"

If your own people can't explain what your company stands for, how can you expect customers or partners to believe it?

In ThinkLab's work with office furniture dealers, we go through a simple exercise that drives this point home. We ask every client-facing employee: "What three words describe what makes your brand truly unique?" The answers, gathered anonymously from a dozen different companies, are turned into word clouds, with one representing each of the twelve different organizations. (See Figure 7.1 for some examples.) The larger the words in the cloud, the more frequently they came up in our discussions. Then, we hang all the word clouds on a wall and invite leaders to pick which one belongs to their organization.

Here's what happens almost every time: Most can't do it. Why? Because the word clouds all look the same. Most are filled with generalities that are hard to back up with actions or proof points. Worse yet, some are able to select their own, but they look the same to the rest of the world.

And here's the kicker: The image above is a *visual* representation of what potential employers *sound like* to most candidates in the interview process—and what product pitches sound like to B2B buyers. Without forming a distinct and memorable identity, they don't stand out from the competition.

Figure 7.1 Responses to the question "What three words describe what makes your brand truly unique?" reveal a surprising pattern—most organizations use the same words to describe themselves.

Source: ThinkLab.Design Dealer Workshop / with permission of ThinkLab.

Now, think back to the brands we've discussed in this chapter. What three words would describe them?

- **Jeep:** Adventure, Culture, Individuality
- **Patagonia:** Sustainability, Integrity, Environmentalism
- **Atlassian:** Transparency, Collaboration, Team-Driven

Even if you don't work at these companies, you know what they stand for—and you can see how that clarity shapes authentic behavior that builds trust both internally and externally.

So, what's the action step? Poll your employees. Do this same exercise with your own team. Then, as a leadership group, decide what three simple words you want to stand for—to guide your culture internally and your brand externally—and use them to shape decisions in every department, from who you hire to the products you make. Once you know what you stand for, the next challenge is making sure that promise shows up consistently—everywhere someone encounters your brand.

Ways to do so:

- **Audit every digital doorway.** Look at your website, your social media channels, Glassdoor reviews, and even the LinkedIn profiles of individual employees. Do they tell the same story? Do they feel like the same company? Do they support your brand message?
- **Trust is in the follow-through.** If you commit to sustainability, share the steps and progress you're making. If you miss the mark, own it publicly. Follow-through earns more trust than a flashy marketing page can.

Idea #2: Be Real, Not a Highlight Reel

While people once preferred polish, today "too perfect" feels unbelievable. People are looking for the real real—not the perfectly staged version. They trust brands that show a little of the mess—the learning, the setbacks, and the behind-the-scenes moments that make them human.

We hear this from designers all the time when they talk about product brands. Today, they trust the companies that are transparent enough to say, "Don't install the flooring this way—we've tried it and here's how it failed," or "Here's where a project was messed up and what you can learn from our mistake." That kind of humility and honesty creates far more loyalty than a glossy brochure ever could.

Here are a few ways to bring this idea to life:

- **Share lessons learned—not just success stories.**
  Internally, that means leaders talk openly about what didn't work and what they learned, creating psychological safety for teams to experiment and for younger generations to share without fear.
  Externally, it means being transparent with customers and partners when things don't go as planned.
- **Respond like a human.**
  Internally, that means leaders answering tough questions honestly instead of hiding behind corporate language.
  Externally, it means giving real answers to clients and partners—even when the answer isn't perfect.

- **Make recognition personal, not performative.**
  Internally, that means noticing and appreciating contributions in real time—not just at review cycles or in all-hands meetings. A simple, specific "thank you" from a leader is more authentic than a generic shout-out slide.
  Externally, it means giving credit to partners, clients, or collaborators publicly. When you highlight others instead of taking all the credit, it signals humility and reinforces that you value relationships over ego.
- **Model and encourage authenticity.**
  Internally, that means making sure HR, marketing, and leadership are working together so the experience you create for employees matches the image you project to clients and partners. *Externally*, empower employees to post, comment, and share their real experiences online. Today, people trust people more than they trust logos. When employees speak in their own voices, credibility grows from the ground up.

When a company is willing to be this open—about mistakes, about the messy middle, about giving credit where it's due—it sends a clear signal: "You can believe us." Authenticity isn't just a marketing tactic; it's a behavior you can cultivate. And when it shows up consistently inside the company, it naturally spills out into how customers, partners, and even future employees experience the brand. The result? Trust that feels earned, not engineered.

Idea #3: Create Space to See and Be Seen

In a recent ThinkLab session with Gen Z employees, we asked how they build trust with their coworkers. Their first answer— "See and be seen"—caught us off guard. Not because the phrase itself was surprising, but because of what they meant by it. For older generations, "See and be seen" usually referred to being physically in the same room. For Gen Z, it's broader than that. Digital also counts. Simply turning cameras on during a virtual meeting helps them feel present with one another, even while miles apart. Seeing faces— expressions, reactions, and real life happening in the background— helps them feel connected.

Cameras on cultures should be a modeled behavior. And whether it's a video call or a thoughtfully designed in-person gathering, these small moments of visibility send a powerful message: "We value you enough to really see you."

When people feel seen, they feel valued. And feeling valued builds trust.

The Future of Trust

For a long time, leadership was about knowing the answers, projecting confidence, and keeping everything looking perfect. But the world has changed. Employees, customers, and partners have access to more information than ever—and they know when the surface doesn't match what's underneath.

We're in the middle of a fundamental shift:

FROM: Trust in management is a given.

Leaders are expected to have all the answers, never admit mistakes, and project certainty and polish above all else.

TO: Trust is something co-created.

Good leaders now ask more questions than they answer. Authenticity has become the new authority. Trust grows when a company is clear about what it stands for, consistent in how it shows up online and in person, and courageous enough to invite others into the process.

The leaders and companies who will thrive in the future will be the ones who practice the ideas in this chapter: clarity about who they are, consistency in how they show up, authenticity in how they communicate, and connection that makes people feel seen.

Looking Ahead: A Glimpse of 2050

If we start building cultures of authenticity and transparency now, what might trust look like a generation from today?

Imagine a world where trust isn't something leaders earn through humility. Credibility comes from being honest about what's still uncertain and being willing to rethink and unlearn. In this future, leaders don't hide behind polish or perfection—they invite feedback, share what they're learning in real time, and stay grounded in consistency even when plans shift. Employees and clients alike can see not just what's promised, but the integrity of how it's pursued.

Leaders no longer earn trust through polish or hierarchy, but through visible consistency. The best brands—and the people who lead them—build credibility by showing their work: inviting feedback, owning mistakes, and proving alignment between words and action.

In 2050, authenticity isn't a choice or a strategy. It's the default currency of trust.

So What? Key Takeaways from Chapter 7

This second shift—from authority to authenticity—isn't just about leadership style. It's a reset on how trust is built.

- **Clarity beats polish.** Know what you stand for and make it simple enough that everyone inside your company can say it—and live it.
- **Consistency is proof.** Align how you show up on your website, on LinkedIn, in a client meeting, and in the hallway so the experience matches the promise.
- **Authenticity is the new authority.** Share lessons learned, respond like a human, and give credit where it's due. People trust the real real, not a highlight reel.
- **Connection builds trust.** Create intentional spaces—both digital and in person—where people feel seen and valued across generations and silos.
- **Trust is co-created.** Leaders set vision and expectations, but trust grows when everyone helps shape the path forward.

In a world where everyone can see behind the curtain, trust isn't mandated from the top-down. It's built—from the inside out.

8

Shift 3

From "We Need" to "You Belong": How to Recruit with Purpose and Impact

> **The big idea:** In a world where employees expect purpose and personalization from day one, the companies that win aren't running longer hiring processes—they're running smarter ones. The best recruiting today builds trust, clarity, and connection from very first click.

BY THE TIME Emily shut her laptop, it was 9:15 p.m.

As a corporate recruiter, she'd spent the day juggling interviews, chasing down feedback, and sorting through the results of multiple different personality tests before she could move any candidates forward. The time and effort for every step of the recruiting process had doubled: more tests, more decision-makers, and, especially, more interviews. She used to conduct five or six interviews for each candidate, but the number of interviews had now swelled to nearly a dozen.

Her inbox was a flood of unanswered candidate emails, each one a reminder of how far behind she was slipping. She wasn't willingly ignoring these emails—she was drowning in them. Lately, she felt less like a recruiter and more like an overworked administrator, buried in twice the work with half the staff.

Emily is an illustration, but the experience today is not uncommon. And this lack of communication is exactly what's damaging trust with the next generation in the recruiting process. According to a recent study, more than 40 percent of Gen Z candidates say companies aren't clear about salaries, 38 percent find job descriptions too vague, and nearly a third say hiring timelines are unclear.[1]

Now, let's consider the flip side of this perspective through Jada, a fictional stand-in for today's Gen Z candidates, informed by the conversations we've had with next-gen job hunters: On the other side of that same recruiting process, Jada sat waiting by her phone. For her, as for many of her peers, this lack of communication wasn't just frustrating—it seemed to be sending a message. She had prepared for weeks for this opportunity, showing up again and again through five rounds of interviews (so far). Each time she left more convinced this was her chance to finally escape her current job, where she felt invisible and undervalued.

This job posting had felt different from the start. While most others read like corporate boilerplate, this one spoke directly to her—not just about the tasks she would perform, but about the impact she could have. That's what she wanted: to wake up in the morning and feel like she was part of something bigger, something that went beyond just earning a paycheck.

And now? Silence.

The Hiring Paradox: More Effort, Less Trust

The recruitment process is often the first opportunity for employer and employee to assess each other and begin developing mutual trust. But today's process often squanders that opportunity. Candidates hope to see a company's words and actions align but instead feel strung along as recruiters schedule yet another interview, pile on tests, and ask candidates to prove themselves again and again. By the time an offer is made—or not made—the delays and miscommunication have tested whatever measure of trust there was.

And the numbers bear this out: Hiring teams conduct 42 percent more interviews per hire in 2024 than they did in 2021 (20 vs. 14), stretching time to hire from 33 to 41 days.[2] But despite the much longer time frame, 61 percent of U.S. job seekers report being ghosted by recruiters—a nine point jump in less than a year.[3] These statistics suggest Gen Z isn't alone in struggling with this problem.

The process is more exhausting than ever on both sides—and ironically, all this additional effort still doesn't guarantee a higher quality of matches.

This disconnect between Jada and Emily isn't just frustrating—it's all too familiar. Everyone's trying their best: the recruiters who are stretched thin, the candidates who are jumping through hoops, both sides hoping for a better outcome. But the process is breaking down. Not because people don't care, but because many of us are still following outdated assumptions that no longer serve today's talent or today's business needs.

The good news: There *is* a better way. Forward-thinking companies are reimagining recruiting—not as a rigid checklist to fill a desk, but as a thoughtful match between skills, impact, and timing. It starts with how best to describe an opening in a job post: less as a laundry list of requirements and more focused on purpose, belonging, and the value someone can bring to the role.

Myth Busting: Why the Old Rules of Recruiting Aren't Working Anymore

For decades, recruiting has been built on a few unspoken assumptions. But the cracks in that thinking are starting to show. Let's bust some of the myths that still shape how most companies recruit today.

Myth #1: More Interviews Mean Better Hires

If that were true, today's marathon hiring processes would be producing dream teams. Instead, they're producing burnout—on both sides of the table. The best candidates are dropping out halfway through or taking prompter offers elsewhere.

Myth #2: Corporate Speak Attracts Great People

Generic job postings that read like they follow a template don't inspire anyone. The best candidates want to know: "How will I fit? Where will I make an impact? And why should I invest my time here?" A posting that answers those questions directly stands out instantly.

Myth #3: Digital Recruiting Means Less Personal Connection

As our research shows, next-gen candidates looking to explore a new company are much more likely to look online first than previous generations. In fact, for each successive generation, we see a greater shift toward digital. That could mean, among other things, browsing the company website, reading Glassdoor reviews, or looking to make connections with current employees on LinkedIn.

Gen Zers are now evenly split between starting the process online vs. with a real, live human (50 percent). Meanwhile, 58 percent of millennials prefer humans first, compared with Gen Xers at 73 percent and boomers at 81 percent. (See Figure 8.1.)

But digital doesn't have to mean bland or impersonal. In fact, a strong digital presence can make recruiting *more* personal by letting you speak directly to the kinds of people you want to attract—at a scale no recruiter could match one-to-one. Done well, a clear and authentic digital presence naturally draws in the right candidates, filters out those who aren't aligned, and frees your team to focus its time and energy on the candidates who *are* the best fit.

Better Recruiting for Every Generation: Practical Ideas for Leaders and Teams

If the old rules of recruiting are breaking down, it's not just a people problem—it's a business problem. SmartRecruiters' 2025 research makes it clear: Recruiting isn't just a human resources function, it's a critical growth engine. Poor hiring slows revenue, damages customer satisfaction, and weakens brand reputation.[4]

WHAT IS YOUR FIRST STEP TO VET A NEW COMPANY YOU ARE CONSIDERING WORKING FOR?

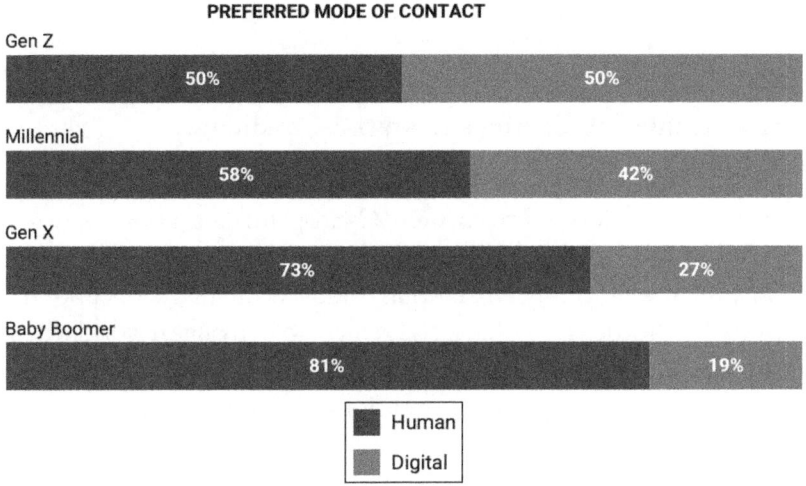

PREFERRED MODE OF CONTACT

Gen Z
| 50% | 50% |

Millennial
| 58% | 42% |

Gen X
| 73% | 27% |

Baby Boomer
| 81% | 19% |

■ Human
■ Digital

Figure 8.1   Each generation is moving more digital in how they explore new companies. Gen Z is evenly split between starting online or with a real person—while older generations still prefer human connection first.

And the stakes are rising. With boomers retiring en masse and too few Gen Xers to fill the gap, millennials and Gen Z are stepping into key roles earlier than ever. If your people are your advantage, everything starts with effective recruiting, which ensures the members of your talent pipeline have strong upward potential.

The good news? The very generation entering the workforce—the one that often frustrates leaders with its new expectations—is also showing us how to fix it. Gen Zers grew up in a world of constant feedback, transparency, and digital connection. They're telling us, with their actions and words, exactly what makes them feel valued and what pushes them away.

And while the following ideas are shaped by a next-gen perspective, they don't just apply to Gen Z. These strategies make recruiting better for everyone—because the appeal of clarity, connection, and purpose is universal.

Here are five ways to start shifting from a transactional model to a more dynamic, future ready approach to recruiting.

Idea #1: Reframe Job Postings from the Candidate's Point of View

One of the clearest lessons from Gen Z? Stop talking about *yourself*, and start talking to *them*.

In Chapter 3, we introduced Hannah Grady Williams' concept of the "NarcisStory"—the idea that Gen Z has grown up in a digital world where everything feels customized to them. It means they want to know where *they* fit in the story you're telling. Traditional job descriptions focus on the "we": *We've* been in business 50 years. *We* pride ourselves on quality. *We're* looking for someone who will join us in doing what we do.

Here's the shift: Flip the language from "we" to "you." Write postings like you're speaking directly to one person.

- Instead of "We need five years of experience in data analytics," try "If you're excited by the way numbers can tell stories and you want to make a visible impact on big decisions, this is your place."
- Instead of "Essential Responsibilities," say "About Your Role with ThinkLab."
- Instead of "Keys to Success," say "How You Will Make a Difference."

Why does this work? Because, as our research shows, Gen Zers want more than just a job. They want purpose, belonging, and clarity on how their contributions matter. We tried this at ThinkLab and attracted double the applicants in half the time when compared to our previous method. These expectations are a wake-up call to modernize how we describe work—and meeting them doesn't just benefit Gen Z. Candidates at every stage of their career want to know: "What impact can I have? How will I fit in?"

The truth is, when you frame a job from the candidate's point of view, you don't just attract next-gen talent—you attract people of every generation who want to be part of something bigger than just checking off a list of requirements.

Idea #2: Make Digital Tools Your Recruiting Superpower

Prepare for Gen Zers to form their first impression of your company online. After all, according to our research, they are more likely than any previous generation to do so.

Done well, it lets you show candidates who you are before your first conversation:

- **Use video intentionally.** Go beyond the polished corporate reel and show what it's really like to work at your company. (We discussed why in Chapter 7!) Focus on simple, real moments: a casual tour of the office or a quick "what I love about my job" video from a team member. Share these authentic, unfiltered "day in the life" videos on public platforms like YouTube, LinkedIn, or Instagram—go where your ideal candidates already are. These honest glimpses help candidates picture themselves as part of your team.
- **Experiment with new formats like Tik Tok résumés.**[5] Invite candidates to submit 60- to 90-second video intros on why they're a match. A simple example might sound like: "Hi, I'm Amanda, and I'm applying for the role of X. Here are three reasons I'm a good fit." These short clips give recruiters a quick, authentic look at communication skills, initiative, and how well a candidate understands what the company is looking for. It's a modern filter that goes far beyond a paper résumé.

These digital-first strategies don't just attract Gen Z. They speed up your process, help your team focus on the most aligned candidates, and create a recruiting experience that feels *more* human—not less.

Idea #3: Broaden Your Talent Model

The next generation of workers doesn't expect a career to follow a straight trajectory—and companies shouldn't, either. Gen Zers value flexibility in how, when, and where they work. They want to make an impact quickly, and are open to portfolio careers that combine projects, contracts, and full-time work. That means the best teams of the future won't be built from full-time roles alone.

Instead of defaulting to a "one-size-fits-all" job posting, start with three simple questions:

1. **What roles can AI now fill?** Offload repetitive, data-heavy tasks so humans can focus on strategy, creativity, and relationships.
2. **What functions are best handled by a contractor?** Short-term or project-based specialists bring in skills you don't need on staff year-round.
3. **What roles are best suited for full-time employees?** Reserve these for work that requires deep cultural alignment, collaboration, and long-term growth.

Gen Z's influence here is important: Building a dynamic talent model opens doors for all generations—parents caring for young kids, semi-retired experts, or anyone at any age looking for a different pace—while also making your company more resilient.

When you start thinking this way, recruiting becomes less about filling one role forever and more about building the right team for now—and for what's next.

Idea #4: Replace Marathon Interviews with "Try Before You Buy"

Once you've used digital tools to narrow the pool to the strongest candidates, the most effective next step isn't more interviews—it's more interaction. The truth? You don't need another round of conversation. As many learn the hard way, likability doesn't always translate into "can do the work."

Invite your top finalists to collaborate with you on a small, paid project. You'll see how they think, how they communicate, and how quickly they "get it." For some roles, you may even consider a contract-to-hire project or period of time if the candidate is willing.

This is more likely to appeal to Gen Z, which is already known for its entrepreneurial mindset. According to a Deloitte report, 46 percent of Gen Z workers in the United States are participating in the gig economy.[6]

This approach flips the focus from "Tell me about your skills" to "Show me how you work." A few months of working together can be more telling for both parties than any résumé or interview process. And, although it aligns naturally with Gen Z's style, it's a modern approach to evaluating fit that works for any role or generation.

Idea #5: Use AI to Close the Feedback Loop—and Free Recruiters to Do What Humans Do Best

For Gen Z, waiting in silence for a reply feels worse than hearing "No, we're not interested." They've grown up in a world of instant feedback: likes, clicks, views, and notifications. So, when weeks go by with no update during a recruiting process, it's more than frustrating. It erodes trust and makes them assume the worst.

AI can help solve this problem. Automated tools can give candidates quick updates, answer common questions, and provide timelines without creating more work for an already overloaded recruiting team. Even a simple "We haven't forgotten you" message keeps candidates engaged and shows respect for their time.

The bigger payoff: By automating repetitive tasks, AI frees recruiters to focus on the human side of hiring—the conversations, the listening, and the thoughtful matching that no algorithm can replicate.

While these changes are shaped by Gen Z expectations, they make recruiting better for everyone. Clear updates, less waiting, and more time for human connection isn't just a nextgen preference—it's universal.

The Future of Recruiting

This shift comes down to a reframe:

FROM: Recruiting is transactional.

Hiring focuses on matching résumés to requirements and assessing likability in interviews. There are limited ways to assess long-term potential or true culture fit.

TO: Recruiting is dynamic.

Companies match talent not just for *now*, but for what's next. That means thinking critically about what AI can do, what's best handled by contractors, and when it's worth investing in full-time roles. The goal is to align opportunity with both company priorities and where a candidate is in their journey—whether it's for a reason, a season, or a long-term path. The process is more purposeful, focused on mutual value and future potential.

Looking Ahead: A Glimpse of 2050

If we follow this path, what might 2050 look like? Let's take a moment to imagine one version of a better future. By 2050, recruiting could look nothing like it does today—and maybe that's a good thing.

Outdated résumés and marathon interviews could give way to dynamic talent profiles—video introductions, interactive portfolios, and AI-powered simulations that reveal how someone thinks, communicates, and collaborates. Intelligent tools could surface best-fit candidates based on values, skills, and potential—not just past titles. For companies, the shift could mean faster, smarter hiring.

And for individuals? The experience could potentially feel *more* human, not less. No more ghosting. No more guessing games. Candidates might have visibility into timelines, pay ranges, and growth paths from day one, helping them to see where they fit—and where they can grow. Roles could flex with their life stage, whether that means project work, part-time impact, or long-term career building.

In this version of the future, the idea of a "job description" will feel archaic. Instead, job descriptions will evolve into value propositions. The best companies won't just ask, "Do you meet our requirements?" They'll want to know: "Where can we grow together?" And the best candidates will stay where they feel a mutual investment in their personal growth.

Most importantly, transparency won't be a buzzword—it will be a baseline expectation. From clear timelines and compensation to well-designed onboarding experiences, the candidate journey could become an early signal of a company's culture, not an exception to it.

Gen Z's demand for purpose, feedback, and flexibility could be the *spark* that helps us rebuild recruiting into something more human, more scalable, and more ready for what comes next for all generations—if we choose to act on it.

So What? Key Takeaways from Chapter 8

This shift—from transactional hiring to purposeful, human-centered recruiting—isn't just a Gen Z demand. It's a signal that the old rules no longer serve today's talent or today's business needs. If we aren't careful, the very place we should be starting from to *build trust* between employee and employer is the very place it's starting to *break down*.

- **Trust starts at the job posting.** Recruiting isn't just a funnel—it's the first impression. Clarity, consistency, and communication signal who you are before a candidate ever clicks "Apply."
- **"We need" is out. "You belong" is in.** The best job descriptions specify where candidates will make an impact—not just what the company needs from them. It's not about requirements; it's about resonance.
- **Digital *can* be personal.** A strong digital presence isn't cold—it's connective. Videos, honest content, and transparent info help the right candidates self-select, saving time and building trust.
- **Interviews don't always equal insight.** More rounds don't mean better hires. Try-before-you-buy models like paid projects or contract-to-hire give both sides a clearer picture—faster.
- **Flexibility is the future.** Full-time roles are just one piece of the puzzle. Smart companies are building agile teams that combine AI, contractors, and long-term hires to meet evolving needs.
- **AI helps humans shine.** Automate the admin, not the empathy. Tools that close feedback loops free recruiters to do what they do best—connect, listen, and build relationships.
- **Gen Z is the spark, not the limit.** Its expectations for purpose and feedback are raising the bar for everyone. Recruiting that works for Gen Z works better for every generation.

9

Shift 4

From Old-School Loyalty to Modern Commitment: The Rules to Retain Have Changed

> **The big idea:** Loyalty isn't dead—it's just more discerning now. In a world where employees have more access to opportunities, options, and information than ever before, the real question isn't "Why are they leaving?" It's "Why would they stay?" People stay where they grow—and leave when their growth stalls.

"GEN Z JUST isn't loyal."

This is one of the most common complaints we heard in our research, from across the spectrum. We heard it from leaders, hiring managers, and even the media. But the Gen Zers we spoke to found this assumption both wrong and offensive.

The data puts the conversation in context. Yes, Gen Z's average job tenure is short.

But let's look at the full picture[1]:

- **Gen Z Average Tenure:** 2 years and 3 months
- **Millennials:** 2 years and 9 months
- **Gen X:** 5 years and 2 months
- **Boomers:** 8 years and 3 months

While job-hopping is a Gen Z phenomenon—it's also a cultural phenomenon happening across every generation today. Tenure is shrinking, and the definition of loyalty is being rewritten in real time.

One moment from one of our Gen Z focus groups captured this perfectly. One Gen Zer told her peers in passing: "I've been here four years. So, a really long time." It wasn't a joke. She was completely sincere. In fact, no one besides me, the Gen X facilitator, even noticed anything remarkable about that statement. The conversation just continued on. It was a reminder for me that in today's workplace—at least for this Gen Z group—four years *is* the new "long time."

The Surprising Truth About Loyalty in an Era of Infinite Options

The real shift? Access. Today, every employee—regardless of age—can benchmark salaries, browse job boards, and receive LinkedIn outreach with just a few taps. And the financial benefits to weighing your options and moving on can be significant. A 2022 McKinsey study found that job mobility pays: On average, workers who changed roles every two to four years gained 30–45 percent more income per move. Those moves explain up to 70 percent of lifetime earnings for upwardly mobile workers, compared with just 30 percent for those who stayed in similar roles.[2]

Given the potential upside, it's no small wonder Gen Zers (and others) are reassessing their expectations for the future and whether or not their current roles offer them the most value.

As one Gen Zer passionately put it: "You say *I* am disloyal? Well, why are you giving me a 3 percent raise when inflation is rising at . . . well, more than that?" This situation was especially galling because, as he noted: "I'm getting outreach from hiring managers suggesting a 10 percent salary increase in my inbox, weekly."

But it's what he said next that really stuck with us. After expressing his frustration, after venting about the numbers, he paused, then shared the one simple request he had for his company: "Give me a reason to stay." That's the new standard. Not tenure for tenure's sake. Just a reason that would make staying worthwhile. That's what these young professionals are searching for today. A sense of progress. A feeling of mutual alignment.

Fittingly, by the time we finished this portion of the study, that participant had left his firm. Also notable is that in the first six months that we met with our 2025 Gen Z Cohort, 25 percent of the participants changed firms. They had no reason to stay, so they didn't.

What we're seeing now is a deeper transformation than mere job-hopping: Loyalty has become transactional, but only when relationships aren't transformational. When people—whether employees or clients—no longer see growth, purpose, or alignment, they don't complain. They simply move on.

When Loyalty Hits a Wall: Two Stories, Two Departures

To dig more deeply into what's happening, let's imagine the following two scenarios. One portrays a common dilemma for employees today, and the other shows what today's business-to-business sales professionals are facing. Both illustrate that what's changing when it comes to loyalty isn't just limited to Gen Z.

Story #1: Olivia Didn't Want to Leave—But Couldn't Afford to Stay

A classic high performer, Olivia was the kind of employee every leader wants—proactive, driven, and deeply committed. But, living in New York, she worried about the rising cost of rent, groceries, and student loans. So, she did what high performers do. She asked her manager for a path forward: "What would it take to become a team lead?"

The response? "You can't rush experience, Olivia." Translation: *Wait your turn.*

But Olivia wasn't asking for a shortcut. She was asking for a road map. Despite her frustration, she remained hopeful—that is, until her next review, when she was offered a raise below the rate of inflation.

That same week, a recruiter reached out with a higher salary bump and a faster growth trajectory. Olivia took the new gig.

But she didn't leave out of disloyalty. She left because no one seemed to care if she stayed.

Now, here's an interesting and real reaction to this fictional story. A Gen X friend who reviewed the book reached out to share her perspective: "More Gen Z graduates are landing six-figure roles without having to prove their worth in the same way we did. Frustrates the sh*t out of me!" We had an intense back-and-forth text exchange about why this frustrated her. By the end of our conversation, she confessed:

> "I will admit that I envy them. They can easily prioritize work–life balance, mental health, and flexibility over traditional career climbing. To older generations, this can read as a lack of 'grind-it-out mentality' or 'less motivated,' but it's a conscious choice to avoid burnout. If I am honest after getting past the anger, I, personally, have struggled all my career in prioritizing me and implementing a more balanced work–life. I want this, too."

So if you, too, are struggling to see past Gen Z "entitlement" as you read this, I encourage you to consider why. And if you, like me and my Gen X friend, also want a better work–life balance, then let's ensure it can happen for not just the younger generations, but us, too. Change starts from within.

Story #2: Jake Stayed Loyal—Until Loyalty Stopped Making Sense

For years, Jake had been loyal to a long-standing furniture dealer that had supported his company through multiple corporate office expansions. He trusted the team and even golfed regularly with his favorite rep.

But pressures changed. Inflation was up, and Jake's CFO wanted every invoice justified. Faced with tightening budgets, Jake did something he hadn't done in years: He put a project out to bid. His current vendor took offense, telling him: "I thought we had a good relationship. Honestly, this feels a little out of the blue."

But the bids Jake received opened his eyes to what else was out there: competitive pricing, faster timelines, more flexible terms. In the end, Jake made the move to a new vendor.

In a world where everything is shifting for knowledge workers—costs, expectations, priorities—*staying relevant* to their lives is what sustains loyalty. Loyalty is no longer guaranteed just because you have a long history of working together. What matters is the present moment—and whether you're still responding to what people actually need. Maintaining loyalty is now a two-way street.

Had Olivia been recognized for her talent and work ethic, she might have decided to be patient and continue on at her original company. Jake was in the market for a new furniture dealer because his company's financial situation had changed, not out of disloyalty. By recognizing that and proactively rethinking discounts or other benefits for this client, the original vendor likely would not have lost Jake as a client to a competitor.

The lesson? Loyalty doesn't disappear out of nowhere. In both cases, these relationships didn't fall apart because of a lack of a "grind-it-out mentality" from Jake or Olivia. They faded because no one realized the goalposts had moved. People don't walk away when they feel understood. They walk away when it feels like no one's paying attention.

Relevance Is the New Retention Strategy

In today's world, where access to opportunities, information, and options are endless, you can't buy loyalty. It has to be earned by aligning with what matters to your employees and your clients. Lose track of that, and you'll lose them.

As one frustrated Gen Z participant told us: "Everyone says Gen Z lacks loyalty, but that's just not true. What we lack is *blind* loyalty."

That's why this shift matters. Because what we're talking about isn't just retention—it's relevance. The era of being loyal *out of obligation* is over. Companies that cling to old assumptions will keep losing top talent and loyal customers—not because people lack commitment, but because they lack a compelling reason to stay. They need to hear a reason that is relevant to their current priorities.

And the data agrees. Yes, pay is still a primary motivator. According to ThinkLab research, across every generation, "higher pay" is the top reason people give for why they'd leave their current role (Figure 9.1). But when we look beyond that, the reasons listed become more personal.

What makes people want to stay? Not just compensation. Not even convenience. But connection. Beyond higher pay, the top three things employees across all generations say they're looking for today are:

1. Supportive coworkers
2. A fun work environment
3. Recognition for their contributions

In other words, it's not the *perks* that motivate them as much as it's the people. It's the culture. It's visibility. Employees are no longer just evaluating roles; these intangibles carry more weight than ever before. Loyalty isn't just about staying—it's about feeling valued and knowing that you can make an impact.

WHAT WOULD TEMPT YOU TO LEAVE YOUR CURRENT ROLE?   *7l.*

	Gen Z	Millennial	Gen X	Baby Boomer
1	Higher pay	Higher pay	Higher pay	Higher pay
2	More flexibility to choose where I work	More flexibility to choose where I work	Nothing	Nothing
3	More flexibility to choose when I work	Better career development	More purposeful work	More purposeful work
4	More interesting work	More flexibility to choose when I work	Better career development	More interesting work
5	More vacation time	More interesting work	Moe interesting work	More flexibility to choose when I work

Figure 9.1   While higher pay is the leading reason employees across all generations would leave their role, secondary motivators differ by generation.

Source: ThinkLab.design Gen Z research / with permission of ThinkLab.

How to Turn Relevance into Retention: Actionable Ideas for Leaders and Teams

Retaining top talent today isn't about ping-pong tables, beer taps, or free lunches. When leaders invest in helping employees of all ages build skills, shape their path, and see a future inside the organization, loyalty follows.

The ideas that follow translate that insight into action—showing how to turn relevance into retention.

Idea #1: Shift from Succession Planning to Success Planning

Traditional succession planning focuses on who will fill a role *someday*. But Gen Zers want to grow *now*. To them, "putting in the time" feels like sitting on the sidelines. They want to design a path for themselves that feels personal, purposeful, and possible.

In one of our ThinkLab brainstorm sessions, we were discussing succession planning when one Gen Z participant grimaced. I paused the conversation to ask why. The participant admitted, "Succession planning just sounds . . . icky. It feels transactional and sterile—like it's about the company, not a real person."

Then, as she kept talking, she unintentionally used the words "success planning," instead of "succession planning." Everyone laughed, but that slip shifted the entire mood of the conversation. Heads nodded in agreement, and every Gen Z participant in the virtual room seemed to feel relief. There was this collective sense of "*Yes*. That's what it should feel like."

Jonathan Webb, Director of Workplace Strategy at KI and one of our manufacturer participants, was observing the session and later shared his reaction:

> "That was a cool moment—and honestly, a major mindset shift for me. I'd never thought about how even our language can feel company-first instead of people-first. 'Success planning'—that just hit different. It felt empowering."

What if a simple shift in language could make growth feel like a shared goal—one that benefits both the company and the individual?

Because when people feel seen and supported, they don't just stay. They thrive.

Idea #2: Upskill Them for Their *Next* Job (So They'll Want to Stay in This One)

It sounds counterintuitive, but it works: The more you help Gen Z prepare for their *next* job, the more likely they are to stay in their *current* one.

In fact, recent studies show a clear link between upskilling or reskilling programs and turnover: A 2025 report by the World Economic Forum found that companies offering upskilling opportunities retain significantly more employees compared to those that do not.[3]

This generation was raised to be in constant learning mode—with access nearly since birth to skill-building content at their fingertips. If your organization doesn't offer growth, Gen Zers will find it elsewhere. (More on this in Chapter 15.) But when companies actively invest in their development, it sends a different message: "You don't have to leave to level up." And maybe even "Go ahead and look around, because you won't find better than this elsewhere."

Whether it's about client management, AI tools, storytelling, or cross-functional know-how, skill-building should feel accessible, exciting, and ongoing—not tied to a job title but tied to potential. Upskill them for what's next, and they'll bring that growth mindset right back into the work they're doing today.

Idea #3: Cross-Pollinate to Keep Things Fresh

Learning doesn't just take place in training modules. It happens in conversations, in shadowing, in unexpected collaborations. When people get exposure to new teams or projects, it helps them grow—and stay connected to the bigger picture.

In ThinkLab research, we tasked Gen Zers with helping solve real business challenges plaguing leaders today. To that end, we asked them directly to share what would make them stay at their organization. What stood out to us in these conversations: They were hungry for visibility into other parts of the company—not just to build skills, but to figure out which skills they *want* to develop and which career path they might want to pursue (and which they don't).

For them, cross-pollination wasn't just interesting—it was motivating. It made them feel more connected to the company and its culture. Here are some ideas for giving them greater exposure:

- **Run "internal residencies."** Let employees spend two to four weeks embedded with another team or client group to gain a new lens and share ideas. It builds empathy, surfaces unexpected solutions, and helps people see how their work fits into the bigger mission.
- **Cross-pollinate project teams.** Break out of silos by intentionally mixing departments or experience levels on high-impact projects. Not only does it diversify thinking—it gives employees a hands-on look at different workflows and leadership styles.

Sometimes, the best way to spark growth isn't a new role—it's a new perspective.

Idea #4: Practice Extreme Transparency

Another idea generated by our Gen Z problem solvers was around pay transparency.

Most companies treat pay like a secret—vague ranges, unclear criteria, and closed-door decisions. But Gen Zers aren't buying it. They don't want to guess what it takes to grow.

They want to see how roles, skills, and contributions connect to compensation and opportunity. And when done right, that sort of transparency motivates everyone—whether through competition, opportunity, or simply by charting a visible path to progress.

Companies like Buffer and Compt are showing what's possible with "extreme transparency": They are not only publishing salary ranges, but also openly sharing the logic, process, and formulas behind how pay is determined. Buffer, for example, doubled job applications in the first month after sharing their salary formulas.[4] Compt saw a 92 percent employee retention rate and a 100 percent close rate with candidates who initially tried to negotiate—only to realize the process was already fair.[5]

Across the board, transparency boosts trust. It reduces turnover. This doesn't just help Gen Z—it improves morale and mitigates pay gaps for all. To put it simply, if you want to keep your best people, don't make them guess the rules of the game. Show them the playbook.

Side note: Beware! Transparency without context can backfire.[6] If employees don't understand the "why" behind pay differences, it can create confusion or resentment. Be sure that when you share the numbers, you also carefully communicate the process and principles behind them.

The Future of Loyalty

The strategies in this chapter are designed for today, but they also point toward a larger shift already unfolding. As each chapter in Section III shows, we're tracking the move from outdated assumptions to emerging realities. The transformation at the heart of this rule is:

FROM: Loyalty means employees prove commitment through years of service.

- Employees stay, grow, and retire at the same company.
- Retention is about stability.
- Job-hopping signals disloyalty.

TO: Loyalty flows both ways.

- Careers are built in chapters, not lifetimes.
- Retention depends on mutual investment, progress, and purpose.
- People stay where they grow—and leave when their growth stalls.

For an example of what all this means, think back to the two stories that appeared earlier in this chapter:

Rising star Olivia was dedicated to her job but left because her company couldn't show her a future worth staying for.

Jake cut ties with a long-time vendor, but not because he stopped caring about their relationship. He left because the vendor lost focus on what mattered to him *now*.

In both cases, the business relationship was no longer mutually beneficial. Feeling that their loyalty was not being reciprocated, Olivia and Jake moved on.

Looking Ahead: A Glimpse of 2050

If this shift continues, what could loyalty look like in 2050?

Imagine a workplace where careers are structured more like well-designed programs: Each role equals one chapter, and each chapter has a beginning, a purpose, and a meaningful exit.

- **Onboarding and offboarding become transformational moments.** Starting a role feels like entering a learning cohort; leaving one feels like graduating—with support, reflection, and continued connection.
- **Career growth is visible, flexible, and self-directed.** Like a choose-your-own-adventure experience, people select growth tracks based on curiosity and contribution—not just tenure or hierarchy.
- **Alumni networks become strategic assets.** Companies build lifelong relationships with former employees, welcoming them back, learning from them, and even turning them into future clients or brand ambassadors.

In this vision of the future, retention won't be about keeping people forever. It'll be about making their time count—and keeping the door open for them to return when the next chapter aligns.

So What? Key Takeaways from Chapter 9

The best way to earn retention today? Make people feel seen, supported, and set up for progress.

- **Loyalty isn't blind anymore.** Gen Zers don't lack loyalty—they lack a reason to give it blindly. Their loyalty is earned through relevance and reciprocity.
- **Growth is the glue.** If people don't see progress, they'll assume it's time to move on. Help them grow, and they'll stick around for the next chapter—not just the next paycheck.
- **Make success personal.** Ditch the one-size-fits-all development plans. Co-create success plans that align with each person's goals, strengths, and next steps.
- **Upskill as a retention strategy.** The more you help people prepare for what's next, the more likely they are to buy in. Invest in their future, and they'll invest in yours.
- **Visibility is the new perk.** Whether it's cross-functional exposure or transparent pay practices, showing people the path forward keeps them motivated to follow it.

10

Shift 5

From Teams to Tribes: Building a Culture of Real Connection

> **The big idea:** We've shifted from culture-as-a-place to culture-as-a-network: a web of microcultures built on trust, shared norms, and belonging. Like strands of a rope, these groups are stronger together, powering performance and keeping people connected no matter where they work.

BEFORE 2020, KNOWLEDGE workers built their team's relationships mostly in one place: the office. We passed teammates in the hallway, caught up over coffee, and shared small, in-person moments that quietly glued us together. Then, almost overnight, our team members transformed into a row of rectangles on a screen.

In some unexpected ways, that shift made us more connected. We saw into each other's worlds: the dog barking in the background, the toddler wandering into frame, the kitchen table doubling as a desk. For the first time, our work and personal lives were fully visible to one another. And when the world reopened, seeing some colleagues in person prompted a surreal moment: "Wait—have we actually met before?"

A Temporary Season, But a Permanent Shift

Today, connection at work no longer depends solely on sharing the same zip code. At a minimum, we need to be able to build a cohesive culture whether or not our teams *are* in the same zip code.

In industries such as architecture and design, teams now routinely form across geographies. An architect in Los Angeles, a designer in Chicago, and a project manager in New York might be paired on a key project and collaborate daily, whether or not they ever breathe the same air. This practice of collaborating remotely existed before 2020, but the past few years both normalized and expanded it.

The same could be said of many other industries. The numbers illustrate how widespread the practice of remote collaboration has become: In 2019, approximately 7 percent of paid workdays were worked remotely; by 2025, that figure increased to 28 percent.[1] Some industries saw over 30 percentage points growth in remote participation from 2019 to 2021 alone, according to the Bureau of Labor Statistics.[2] Together, these trends confirm that forming geo-agnostic, distributed teams isn't just a pandemic blip—it's a structural change in how work gets done.

Even for teams that are fully back in office, evidence shows that collaboration across offices has accelerated in the past decade. For example, a post-pandemic Microsoft study found that about a third of all meetings now include participants from multiple time zones.[3] Additionally, Capterra's 2024 survey on collaboration and productivity found that 59 percent of employees who collaborate with colleagues in other countries have only started doing so within the past two years.[4]

Here's the irony: As so many of us are freed from working at a single set location, the physical office actually matters more, not less. Those spaces now carry greater pressure to spark connection, foster belonging, and strengthen the relationships that make daily collaboration work even after everyone goes back to their separate zip codes.

For many older generations, those bonds still form fastest face-to-face. And even for Gen Z—a generation generally more comfortable building relationships in digital spaces—in-person moments *do* still matter. But face-to-face can't be the only way to build teams and connections in this deeply interconnected world.

The Rise of Microcultures

The strongest expressions of company culture now span a mix of spaces—physical, digital, and in-between—and are forged by smaller, closer-knit groups that act like tribes within the larger organization.

We call these groups "microcultures," and ThinkLab research shows that they are where the tightest bonds are formed. Across every generation, employees say they feel more cared for by their manager than by their company. For Gen Zers, that gap is striking: 57 percent say their manager "always" cares about their well-being, compared to just 32 percent who say the same about their company (Figure 10.1). Responses from millennials are even less favorable: Only 28 percent say their company "always" cares. The loyalty is local.

Gallup data supports this finding: 54 percent of employees with a highly effective manager say they plan to stay at their organization for at least two more years, compared to just 39 percent for those with a less effective one.[5] In other words, the *person* you work for matters just as much as—if not more than—the *company* you work for.

Why Soft Skills Are More Important Than Ever

This puts more pressure than ever on managers to be the glue that holds culture together. It means that developing their ability to lead people isn't optional—it's the lever that holds the whole system up.

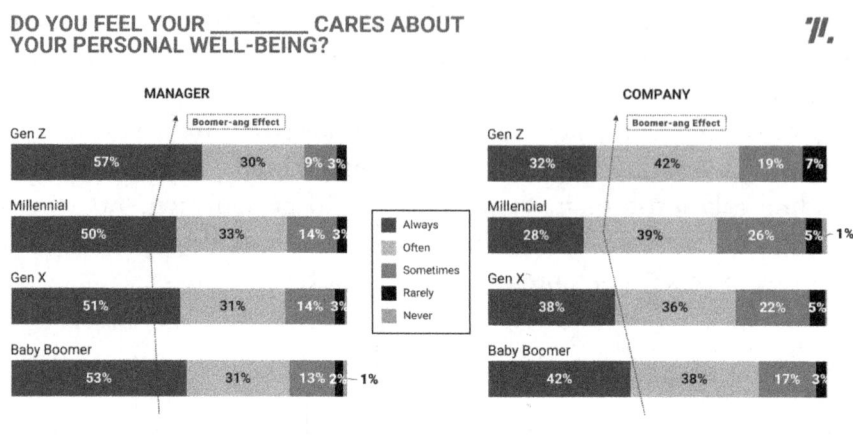

DO YOU FEEL YOUR _____ CARES ABOUT
YOUR PERSONAL WELL-BEING?

Figure 10.1   Connection is built person to person. Employees feel more cared for by their direct managers than by their organizations as a whole.

Source: ThinkLab.design Gen Z research / with permission of ThinkLab.

We've already discussed some of the transformative changes that have made these skills harder to come by: Communication channels have multiplied, teams stretch across time zones and cultures, and AI is adding new layers of complexity to how we work and connect. Solving this problem will take more than simply hosting a workshop. It will take an ongoing commitment to helping managers listen with empathy, adapt their leadership style across generations, and create clarity in the midst of noise.

These are the skills that will differentiate leaders in an increasingly digital workplace—and the faster we equip managers with them, the more resilient, connected, and loyal our tribes will be. Yet the very leaders playing this role are often promoted for technical expertise, not people skills. We often think Gen Zers lack soft skills (and they often do), but the truth is that today, as the context and rules around work shift, all of us need to update our people skills.

Podcast Spotlight: "Generation Gap: Rethinking Soft Skills in the Hybrid Workplace"

This episode of the *Design Nerds Anonymous* podcast features Kendra Johnson, founder of The Venned Group and Canada's leading soft skills expert.

Johnson shares: "Many strong individual contributors get promoted because they excel at their craft. But being good at the thing doesn't automatically make you a great manager, especially when you add the complexities of hybrid work and geographically dispersed teams."[6]

Here is her best advice for managers in today's environment:

- **Start with self-awareness.** Your tone, clarity, and energy set the emotional climate for the team. "Managers are culture carriers," she says. "Your behavior ripples."
- **Proactive beats reactive.** Don't wait for miscommunication to become conflict. Ask questions (such as "How do you like to receive feedback?") to prevent misunderstandings across generations.
- **Recognize the ROI of soft skills.** Johnson shares a story about one client who saved a major account by improving communication, which then unblocked the adoption of a critical project management tool.

For more insights, follow Johnson on LinkedIn. Her practical wisdom on navigating the human side of work is exactly what the next generation of leaders need.

Explore your own soft skill strengths and gaps by listening to this DNA podcast episode.

The Need for Connection Is Universal—But It's Not One-Size-Fits-All

As we've seen from the data, managers are often the primary point of loyalty for employees, but there's more to that story. ThinkLab's research shows that across *every* generation, "supportive coworkers" rank as the #1 driver of workplace engagement (Figure 10.2). The instinct to invest in the people closest to us is a cross-generational constant.

The generations differ when it comes to the factors lower down on the list. Gen Z places slightly more weight on "community engagement" than any other group, and ranks "a challenging work environment" the lowest. (Interestingly, "a challenging work environment" is ranked highest by boomers, and then progressively lower by each successive generation.) These nuances hint at where culture is headed: toward workplaces that prize belonging, inclusivity, and social impact alongside traditional measures of performance.

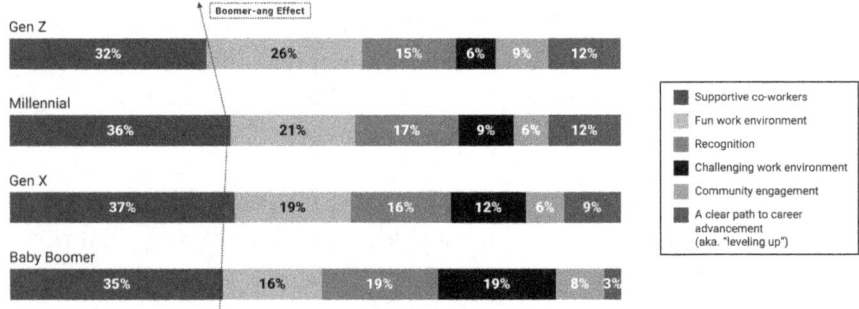

WHICH OF THE FOLLOWING MAKES YOU FEEL
MOST ENGAGED WITH YOUR ORGANIZATION?

Gen Z
Boomer-ang Effect
32% | 26% | 15% | 6% | 9% | 12%

Millennial
36% | 21% | 17% | 9% | 6% | 12%

Gen X
37% | 19% | 16% | 12% | 6% | 9%

Baby Boomer
35% | 16% | 19% | 19% | 8% | 3%

- Supportive co-workers
- Fun work environment
- Recognition
- Challenging work environment
- Community engagement
- A clear path to career advancement (aka. "leveling up")

Figure 10.2   Supportive co-workers rank as the #1 driver of engagement for every generation.

Source: ThinkLab.design Gen Z research / with permission of ThinkLab.

But how that belonging and connection is built can vary widely. When ThinkLab asked employees of all ages for the single best way to build camaraderie, the top answer from Gen Z, millennials, and Gen X was "socializing" (Figure 10.3). But that word means very different things to each generation.

- For Gen Z and millennials, it often refers to a hybrid experience: intentional in-person time, but also quick check-ins on Slack, group texts, and maybe even a spontaneous video chat.
- For Gen X, it still often means literal face time: breathing the same air, sharing experiences, and working side by side.
- Boomers stand apart: They were the only ones whose top answer wasn't "socializing," pointing to a tendency to separate work and personal life, compared to younger generations. Instead, boomers ranked "trust" first, and theirs was the only generation to include "respect" in their top four.

**WHAT SINGLE WORD OR PHRASE DESCRIBES
THE BEST WAY TO BUILD CAMARADERIE
WITH COLLEAGUES?**

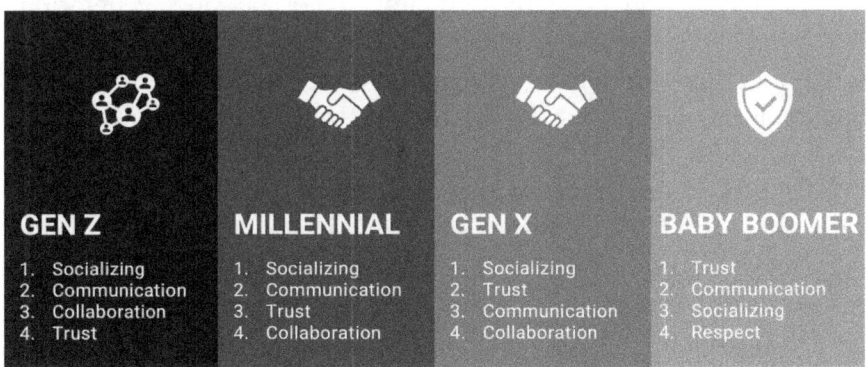

GEN Z	MILLENNIAL	GEN X	BABY BOOMER
1. Socializing	1. Socializing	1. Socializing	1. Trust
2. Communication	2. Communication	2. Trust	2. Communication
3. Collaboration	3. Trust	3. Communication	3. Socializing
4. Trust	4. Collaboration	4. Collaboration	4. Respect

Figure 10.3 Across most generations, "socializing" ranks as the top way to build camaraderie—except for boomers, who prioritize trust above all.

Source: ThinkLab.design Gen Z research / with permission of ThinkLab.

Across all generations, the need for the same building blocks surface, just in a different order. Socializing, communication, trust, and collaboration are crucial to interacting with your coworkers, whether it happens over coffee, via a video camera lens, or in a shared Slack channel.

How to Build Culture Today: Practical Ideas for Leaders and Teams

With teams spread across zip codes, time zones, and even continents, the culture of your organization no longer depends on proximity alone. Instead, it's forged in microcultures: the smaller, trust-filled groups that keep people connected no matter where they sit.

And the stakes are high. When culture is left to chance, miscommunication grows, burnout spreads, and turnover rises. But when culture is intentionally designed, the payoff is clear: stronger collaboration, higher loyalty, and deeper resilience across every generation of the workforce.

The good news? The very pressures that make culture harder to sustain—hybrid schedules, digital overload, and generational differences—also point us toward solutions. Gen Z's comfort with digital connection, millennials' hunger for work–life balance, and Gen X and boomers' desire for stability all reveal what works: flexibility, clarity, and belonging.

And while the following ideas are shaped by a next-gen perspective, they don't just apply to Gen Z. These strategies strengthen culture for everyone—because the appeal of connection, trust, and respect is universal.

What follows are four ways to put that "tribe-building" mindset into practice.

Idea #1: Empower "DDD" Ownership: Discuss, Decide, Document

Culture endures when teams create their own playbook for how they work together. Outlined in the book *How the Future Works*, the "team-level agreement" is a living document that captures the shared norms of a small working team, as opposed to a set of policies from HR.[7] These are co-created guidelines where teams agree on norms such as preferred communication styles and what flexibility means in practice. The goal is to make expectations visible and intentional so they can be honored, adapted, and improved upon over time.

Here's how:

1. **Decide alone.** Before you can join a team-level discussion, you and each member of your team will first need to think through your responses on your own. For help with this, download Future Forum's customizable template.[8] (The link is included in the corresponding footnote.) Or, if you're struggling, refer back to Chapter 3 to help you "enter your era of intentional selfhood" and focus on what *you* need.

2. **Discuss openly.** To start, hold a dedicated session where team members can share preferences, needs, and working styles. Make space for specifics, listing everything from meeting times to preferred feedback channels. We strongly recommend that you work from the customizable template mentioned above. If your core team is working across geographies, this may be a great time to bring them together in person, retreat-style.

3. **Decide together.** Find common ground and set clear expectations. If there's disagreement, aim for workable compromises. Make it clear that everyone will not get everything they want, but together you can find workable solutions.

4. **Document visibly.** Store the agreement where everyone can reference it and revisit it. Update it when circumstances change—the power is in keeping it alive.

When the members of a team define its norms, they help to build a culture that reflects their reality—and strengthens the trust needed to deliver their best work.

Idea #2: Foster Work–Life Respect—With Flexibility That Flows Both Ways

A team agreement sets the framework, but the true test of whether your culture is sustainable comes down to everyday trade-offs. How do you respond when a team member needs to shift hours, step away, or ask for help?

When flexibility flows both ways, it stops being a perk to be guarded and becomes a mutual benefit—one that strengthens loyalty and makes the team more resilient when life inevitably gets messy. Here's how to make flexibility feel fair, not fragile:

- **Normalize real-life transparency.** Create a climate where it's safe to share that you need to log off early or start later because of personal needs. Instead of simply saying "I'm stepping out for an hour," be open about the "why." For example: "I'm leaving at 4 to take my kid to the doctor" or "I'm offline for therapy from 1–2 today." Sharing the human side of our lives helps destigmatize personal responsibilities and gives others permission to balance their own.
- **Balance the give-and-take.** If you need flexibility one week, look for ways to return the favor the following week: Cover a call for a team member, take on an extra task, or swap meeting times. These behaviors build trust among teams. Make reciprocal support an explicit expectation when you create your team-level agreements.
- **Set boundaries in advance.** Define what's flexible and what's not. Decide as a team which commitments can shift (such as meeting times) and which are fixed (such as client deadlines). Clarity removes the guesswork when conflicts arise. For example, I have a consistent half-hour blocked off so I can eat lunch. It's not uncommon for my team members to book over that when *really* needed, but most of the time they respect that I block off that time.

When we know what matters to the people we work with, we develop more empathy, context, and patience that help us weather hard days together. By learning each other's "why," we stop equating teammates with the roles they fill and start seeing them as people worth showing up for.

Idea #3: Make Feedback Frequent, Not Formal

For Gen Zers, waiting a year for an annual review feels like receiving a letter by carrier pigeon. By the time it arrives, it's considered more offensive than helpful: "Why didn't you tell me sooner?" For a generation that grew up with instant ratings, likes, and comments, delayed feedback doesn't just feel old-school; it can feel irrelevant or even disrespectful. And Gen Zers are not alone in feeling this way: Across generations, people do their best work when they know, in real time, how they're doing.

Here's how to keep the feedback loop running:

- **Share the good immediately.** Don't wait for a meeting to acknowledge great work. A quick message or public shout-out reinforces the behaviors you want to see.
- **Address issues in the moment.** A small course correction today is easier (and less awkward) than a major one months later. Keep it specific, constructive, and kind.
- **Supercharge your one-on-one meetings.** Weekly or biweekly one-on-ones are one of the best vehicles for timely, meaningful feedback, but only if they're done well. Research from Steven Rogelberg, author of *Glad We Met: The Art and Science of 1:1 Meetings*, found that most managers never receive training on how to run them.[9] Avoid the biggest traps: letting the manager do most of the talking, using the time for status updates, or skipping them when things get busy. Instead, center the meeting around the employee: Have them set or co-create the agenda, focus on their challenges and goals (not just tasks), and ask open-ended questions such as "What's on your mind?" Close with a recap and clear next steps. Done right, one-on-ones boost engagement, retention, and trust—and become the front line for inclusion and belonging.

When feedback becomes part of your everyday rhythm, it's no longer a dreaded event—it's proof that your team members are paying attention, care about each other's growth, and refuse to let problems fester.

Idea #4: Unlock Your Team's "Working Genius"

One of the most effective ways to strengthen your immediate work team—beyond putting people in the right roles for them—is to understand how they fit together as a team. One tool that we've found powerful at ThinkLab is Patrick Lencioni's *The 6 Types of Working Genius*.[10] It's a simple assessment that identifies what boosts each person's energy and what drains it.

Here's the gist: Each of us has two "genius" areas (what fills your bucket or lights you up), two "competencies" (skills you can do well but don't necessarily love), and two "frustrations" (work that drains you if you do it for long). The model identifies six fundamental activities every team needs to thrive: Wonder, Invention, Discernment, Galvanizing, Enablement, and Tenacity.

When you map a team against this model, patterns emerge. You can see why some duos naturally gravitate toward working together. You can also spot gaps that explain persistent friction, as with a team heavy on generating ideas but light on closing out projects. On our own team, I score high in Innovation and Discernment (I love pulling together research and ideas), but Tenacity is a weak spot for me. Enter my colleague Allison, who thrives on Tenacity and can polish our decks to perfection. (Her running joke: "Yep, we lost Amanda on slide 24 . . .")

This tool not only explains personalities but also helps team leaders design work teams and workflows intentionally. Imagine assigning projects so that your people spend most of their time in their "genius" area, while ensuring the team as a whole covers all six areas. Suddenly, collaboration feels less like conflict and more like chemistry.

When team members learn to recognize each individual's strengths and unique contributions, they get more done with less friction—and they also grow to understand each other better. And that creates a culture where trust grows naturally, because everyone is working from their strengths, in service of the team.

The Future of Microcultures

The ideas in this chapter address today's reality—but they also point to where workplace culture is heading.

FROM: Culture is built from the top-down.

- Leaders set the tone, and the organization's values trickle down through the ranks.
- Loyalty is hierarchical: Employees are loyal to the company.
- Culture change starts with policy.

TO: Culture grows from the inside out.

- The strongest bonds form in microcultures: small, closer-knit tribes inside the larger organization.
- Loyalty is local: Employees are loyal to the people they work with every day.
- Culture change happens in moments, not mandates—through the norms, rituals, and relationships built at the team level.

Looking Ahead: A Glimpse of 2050

If we start investing in microcultures now—equipping managers with people skills, encouraging reciprocal flexibility, and incorporating feedback daily—what might the workplace look like a generation from today?

Imagine it's 2050, and your team spans six countries and four generations, but operates with the cohesion of a close-knit studio. In this vision of the future, every manager has AI tools at their disposal that flag early signs of burnout or disconnection, prompting quick check-ins with their team members. Your "team agreement" lives in an interactive space that updates in real time as needs shift, translating seamlessly across time zones and languages. And personality tools—evolved from earlier models like Patrick Lencioni's *Working Genius*—make it second nature to align projects with people's strengths, ensuring every team has the right balance of dreamers, doers, and finishers.

As they do today, people still choose to stay not out of loyalty to their company, but because of the deep trust and sense of belonging they feel with their immediate work tribe. And those microcultures now weave together into organizations that are more resilient, inclusive, and human than ever before.

So What? Key Takeaways from Chapter 10

This shift—from broad organizational culture to microcultures—is a recognition that loyalty and belonging grow strongest in the small, closer-knit circles we interact with every day. And by intentionally knitting those microcultures together, like strands of a rope, they become stronger than any single one on its own.

- **Culture is no longer tied to zip codes.** Belonging and collaboration now span offices, time zones, and countries—and culture must thrive across all of them.
- **Belonging is a competitive advantage.** It fuels loyalty, performance, and advocacy far more than perks or policies.
- **Loyalty is local.** People stay for the relationships closest to them, especially with their direct managers and coworkers.
- **Intentionality matters.** Microcultures thrive when norms, rituals, and flexibility are designed on purpose, not left to chance.
- **Feedback can't wait a year.** Especially for Gen Z, immediacy is the norm; delayed feedback feels irrelevant, even disrespectful.
- **Soft skills are the hard skills.** In a hybrid, AI-enabled workplace, empathy, great communication, and adaptability are what set great managers apart.
- **Smart tools amplify trust.** New models like *Working Genius* show how personality frameworks can help teams balance strengths, close gaps, and work in ways that energize—not drain—them.

11

Shift 6

From Ladders to Jungle Gyms: The New Rules of Purpose at Work

> **The big idea:** We are at risk of a leadership pipeline crisis because younger generations demand that we define career success differently. Titles, status, or corner offices are no longer the sole motivators. Instead, Gen Zers set a premium on purpose and autonomy—and prioritizing their well-being along the way.

A FRIEND OF mine was on a college visit with his son at Wake Forest University when a professor shared a ritual that's been part of orientation since the 1950s. Every year, incoming freshmen answer the same question: "How many of you believe you're destined for the C-suite?"

For more than six decades, the response was remarkably stable. Year after year, only about 25 percent of students raised their hands. But starting around 2020, something shifted. From that point on, nearly two-thirds of students raised their hands—and the number has stayed high ever since.

Of course, the parents that day were shocked by this statistic. You might be tempted to shake your head as well. This new level of confidence feels almost presumptuous. But then, the professor added a twist to the original question: "How many of you, as parents, ask your kids where they want to go on vacation?" Almost every hand went up in response.

Then as a follow-up, he pressed, "How many of you were consulted about family vacations when you were children?" Barely any parents raised their hands.

The room fell quiet. The point was clear: These kids didn't simply decide, out of the blue, to expect a say. They were raised to have one. And that expectation isn't limited to giving their opinions on family vacations—it's redefining how they view leadership itself.

Why Traditional Leadership Roles No Longer Appeal

But here's the paradox: According to Deloitte's 2025 study on Gen Z and millennials, only 6 percent of Gen Zers say leadership is their primary goal when they're asked directly.[1] Yet, as we saw at Wake Forest, more students than ever indicate that they see themselves destined for the C-suite—they've been raised to believe they *deserve* a voice.

In other words, Gen Zers think they have what it takes to be in the C-suite, but they aren't going there. Why? They're clearly confident enough to imagine themselves at the top of their field. Perhaps that same confidence is what empowers them to turn down the opportunity if it no longer seems worth it. They're looking at the playbook older generations are following, and they aren't signing up. A recent Glassdoor piece found that 68 percent of Gen Z workers said they wouldn't pursue management if it weren't for the paycheck or title.[2] They're not rejecting leadership itself—they're rejecting what leadership has traditionally required.

A Leadership Pipeline Gap

These statistics point to a looming leadership void.

Forrester has projected that by 2030, Gen Zers and millennials will comprise 74 percent of the global workforce.[3] While Gen Z alone makes up only 27 percent of the workforce in 2025, they are projected to become the dominant generation in the workplace within a decade.[4] Yet, unlike their predecessors, they aren't lining up for the corner office.

The consequences extend far beyond individual career choices. With such a large share of the workforce opting out of the traditional climb, organizations face what Stanton Chase calls a leadership pipeline crisis.[5] Succession plans built around steady hierarchical advancement are breaking down.

After all, many younger workers have seen their parents or older relatives demonstrate strong loyalty and a tireless work ethic to employers, only to face layoffs, reduced benefits, or a lack of reciprocal loyalty—often during recessions or organizational changes. The broad adoption of AI is making them question that job security even more: Roughly 70 percent of Gen Z participants in Glassdoor's recent study felt that way. "Gen Z is reconsidering what it means to be successful at work in this moment," said Daniel Zhao, Glassdoor's chief economist. "They're not rejecting ambition—they're redirecting it toward sustainable career paths that prioritize both financial security and personal fulfillment."

Success Is Not Being Rejected, It's Being Redefined

At the heart of this leadership pipeline gap lies burnout. According to a 2025 study, 66 percent of U.S. workers today are experiencing burnout, an all-time high.[6,7] Younger generations are facing it at significantly higher rates, with 81 percent of 18- to 24-year-olds and 83 percent of 25- to 34-year-olds reporting burnout, compared to just 49 percent of those aged 55 and older. For many rising professionals, advancement no longer looks like opportunity—it looks like exhaustion. "Work–life balance is really important. I feel we say it, but we don't do it," one Gen Z designer told us. "Keeping your mental health, emotional health, physical health—all of that is important for us to continue to be good at what we do."

When the path to leadership demands trading well-being for status, the next generation simply opts out. Not out of laziness or lack of ambition, but due to a fundamental redefinition of success. Where previous generations saw titles, offices, and authority as the pinnacle of their careers, younger workers are chasing something different. Deloitte's 2025 study calls it the "trifecta": meaningful work, financial security, and genuine well-being.

The old model of leadership—long hours, constant availability, and top-down authority—often comes at the expense of balance, flexibility, and health. Instead of chasing prestige, younger workers don't want to compromise the trifecta of what they value most.

Much of ThinkLab's research centers on the interior design industry, historically known for grueling work hours. Our industry-specific research echoes trends in other industries.

What pushes Gen Z out: Four red flags top the list.

1. Lack of work–life balance and flexibility
2. Lack of recognition/visibility
3. Lack of investment in growth (time, coaching, inspiration)
4. Lack of diversity and belonging

Together, these priorities are signals of a generation seeking purpose, respect, and a clear path to contribute. (And don't we all want that?)

What keeps Gen Z in: Make recognition tangible (with credit on client emails, visible wins, etc.), pair early-career talent with buddies/near-peer mentors, give real-time feedback, and design onboarding to teach the culture as much as the job. Invest in education that protects their time by combining self-directed learning with human coaching.

Unless organizations reimagine what leadership looks like, they risk a vacuum at the top.

Podcast Spotlight: "Gamify Career Paths for Gen Z"

So, if the old model of leadership no longer appeals, what comes next? How do we redesign career paths so that ambitious young talent doesn't simply step off the treadmill? That question was at the heart of our episode featuring Rohin Shahi, Gen Z author of the book *The Z Factor: How to Lead Gen Z to Workplace Success*. Shahi argues that the problem isn't that Gen Zers lack ambition—it's that the paths we've built don't line up with what motivates them.

"Traditional career ladders were designed for a different time," Shahi explained. "Gen Z wants to see visible progress sooner, not wait years for a promotion. They thrive when they can track their growth like levels in a game—through skills gained, feedback earned, and milestones reached along the way."[8]

Key insights from our conversation included:

- **Gen Zers see careers like a jungle gym, not a ladder.** Linear paths feel outdated. They want flexible growth, lateral moves, and options that reflect their evolving interests—not rigid timelines.
- **Gamification works, but only when it's meaningful.** Points, perks, and bonuses aren't enough. True engagement stems from a sense of purpose, collaboration, and personal progress, not just competition. Frequent, tangible "wins" keep employees motivated.
- **Transparency is the new trust.** Gen Z wants to know what it will take to reach the next level. Clear expectations, consistent feedback, and visible career paths reduce anxiety and boost motivation.

The takeaway: If companies want to fill tomorrow's leadership bench, they can't rely on the old promise of "Stick around long enough, and you'll move up." They must design careers that feel dynamic, rewarding, and worth engaging in every step of the way.

Explore more ways to gamify career paths by listening to this DNA podcast episode with Gen Z author, Rohin Shahi.

Gamifying growth doesn't just keep talent engaged—it ensures companies don't lose their future leaders before they're even in the running. When people of all generations can see progress and choose their path, they don't disengage. They level up.

Why Career Progression Needs Meaning, Not Fancy Titles

If visible progress keeps younger employees motivated enough to reach the next mini-milestone, *purpose* is what sustains them in the long run. Career "levels" only matter if they lead somewhere meaningful.

We have all inherited this unspoken norm: Purpose is something you find at the top of the ladder; if you climb high enough, fulfillment will follow. But the next generation is flipping that script. Employees aren't waiting until mid-career or executive status to demand purpose. They want it now.

Podcast Spotlight: "Igniting Purpose at Work: Inspiring Employees"

The theme of purpose came through powerfully in this episode featuring Akhtar Badshah, former head of Microsoft's philanthropy program and author of *Purpose Mindset: How Microsoft Inspires Employees and Alumni to Change the World*. Badshah argues that purpose isn't a perk reserved for senior leaders; it must be woven into the DNA of daily work for everyone.

"Purpose doesn't sit on a poster in the hallway. It shows up in the choices organizations make every day," Badshah explained.[9]

Key insights from our conversation included:

- **Purpose fuels performance.** Employees who see meaning in their work show higher levels of engagement and loyalty.
- **Purpose isn't abstract.** It lives through daily tasks and rituals, as well as the tangible ways companies connect contributions to impact.
- **Leadership matters.** Leaders who articulate *why* the work is important ignite deeper commitment across all generations.

In other words, if gamified career paths answer the "how" of growth, purpose answers the "why." And for Gen Z and millennials, both the how *and* the why must work together to redefine what leadership and advancement look like in the years ahead.

Listen to this DNA podcast episode with author Akhtar Badshah here to learn more about how to weave purpose in to work for every generation.

A sense of purpose isn't just about fulfillment—it's the magnet that keeps tomorrow's leaders in the pipeline.

Expanding the Leadership Pipeline: Practical Ideas for Leaders and Teams

The crisis is real: If organizations continue to define leadership as long hours, rigid hierarchies, and sacrifice without recognition, the bench will keep emptying.

But there's also an opportunity: By redesigning leadership itself—around balance, purpose, and progress—we don't just engage the next generation; we create healthier paths that help leaders of all ages thrive today.

Let's take a closer look at four ways to expand the leadership pipeline.

Idea #1: Redefine Leadership Through Well-Being

For too long, advancement has been framed as a trade-off: more responsibility in exchange for less balance, more prestige in exchange for fewer boundaries.

Today's rising leaders are demanding a different model. They're looking to their mentors and managers and asking a simple question: "Does this look like a life I want?" In the *Design Nerds Anonymous* podcast episode on gamifying career paths, Corianne Burrell of Perkins&Will reflected, "It made me realize: Why would someone stay with a company and be motivated to grow into a role if they see it as undesirable? Leaders need to make their jobs look appealing."

When leaders visibly model balance, they signal that well-being is part of the role. That can be as simple as making the following changes:

- **Protect boundaries.** Stop responding to emails outside of agreed-upon working hours or on weekends.
- **Normalize family commitments.** Share openly when you're leaving for a child's baseball game or a parent's doctor's appointment, especially if it's after a grueling travel week.
- **Take rest seriously.** Use your vacation days, unplug fully, and talk about the benefits of doing so when you return.
- **Model health in small ways.** Block time for exercise, mental health, or recovery—and encourage your team to do the same.

Some companies are formally embedding these expectations with great results:

Volkswagen: The German automaker enforces a "Right to Disconnect" policy, where non-management employees are not expected to respond to emails outside of working hours. Between 6:15 p.m. and 7:00 a.m., email access is shut off on their smartphones.[10] This policy is part of a wider European movement aimed at reducing digital overload and respecting work–life balance. Quarterly and yearly financial reports through 2025 continue to show steady revenue and operating profits, indicating that respecting employee work–life balance has not hindered Volkswagen's competitiveness or financial success.[11]

Exos: This U.S.-based fitness company recently published the results from the first six months of its four-day workweek trial.[12] Exos, which employs more than 3,000 people around the world, reported its largest gain in retention after implementing this anti-burnout program. Impressively, it saw its turnover rate drop from 47 percent in 2022 to 29 percent in 2023.

Stryker: This global medical technology company has invested heavily in work–life integration programs, including unlimited paid time off, flexible hours, and hybrid work options. Its strong growth—$22.6 billion in annual revenue and a $140 billion market value in 2024—correlates closely with its people-first strategy. Consistently recognized as one of the world's best workplaces by *Fortune*, Glassdoor, and the Disability Equity Index, Stryker's success suggests that prioritizing employee well-being is not only good for culture but also a driver of retention, talent attraction, and sustained business performance.

If the old leadership model equated advancement with sacrificing personal well-being for the company, the new one must redefine it as sustaining both the work *and* the worker.

Idea #2: Reimagine Career Progression

Traditional career ladders often limit employees to a binary choice: Path A or Path B. In a traditional design firm, for example, you're generally either following the path of designer (the more creative track) or project manager (the more technical one). But Gen Zers don't want to be pigeonholed so soon. They're asking: "What skills can I develop? What new areas can I explore?" Sometimes, they don't even know which questions to ask to help them determine their next steps.

Leaders have an opportunity to reimagine advancement—moving away from the unspoken rule that employees can only climb up the ladder after years of paying their dues. Instead, consider progression in terms of a jungle gym: As you make your way through it, you acquire a new set of skills.

One way to acquire those skills is to create a "chore chart" of stretch tasks. At home, I sometimes post sticky notes for my kids. Clean the bathroom: $5. Take out the trash: $2. Everyone knows what needs doing and what it's worth, and they can choose what to take on. Why couldn't work be the same? Post stretch opportunities—such as drafting a client report, shadowing a sales call, or leading an internal brainstorm—with clear credit or reward. In return, employees gain skills, visibility, and agency.

The key is transparency, choice, and—most importantly—empowerment. When companies gamify skill development with clear milestones and micro-wins, they keep employees engaged day-to-day, while growing the skills pipeline their business will need tomorrow.

Idea #3: Empower Exploration Through ~~Entrepreneurship~~ Intrapreneurship

In parenting, there's a concept called a "see-do" list, which is a departure from the "chore chart" approach we mentioned above. Instead of handing kids a checklist of chores, parents encourage them to notice what needs doing, take initiative, and get it done. Then, they are rewarded for it. It lightens the mental load on parents, who no longer have to script every task—and it empowers kids to develop responsibility and ownership.

The workplace could use more of this. Just as moms often carry the mental load of creating the family chore chart, managers often carry the weight of directing every next step for their teams. What if, instead, employees were encouraged to "see" company challenges and "do" something about them—bringing their own passions, skills, and ideas to bear?

That's the essence of intrapreneurship: channeling employees' varied interests and entrepreneurial energy inward, into projects that directly benefit the company. As Rohin Shahi explained in the previously mentioned podcast episode, "Having an employee who is interested in different things doesn't necessarily mean they're not committed to the job. It just means they have other passions they also want to pursue."

So, let them. Instead of funneling every employee into one of a limited number of paths, harness their drive to power intrapreneurship models. These are structured ways for employees to flex entrepreneurial muscles, experiment, and innovate, all without leaving the company. And just like the "see-do" list, this effort must be rewarded.

That doesn't always have to mean cash. Rewards can be recognition, new opportunities, or even the visibility that comes from leading a project. What matters is that initiative is noticed and valued. Examples include:

- **Start internal innovation labs.** Create forums where employees pitch new ideas for products, services, or processes—and get time and resources to test them.
- **Encourage cross-functional "passion projects."** Let employees apply outside skills (in graphic design, data analysis, social media, etc.) to company initiatives that need fresh energy.
- **Invite diverse voices into problem-solving.** Bring employees from varied roles and backgrounds into sessions to solve key business challenges, then empower them to *execute* the solutions, not just observe.

Supporting intrapreneurship doesn't mean encouraging everyone to build the next big start-up on company time. It means creating project-based opportunities where entrepreneurial energy contributes to the company's goals. Employees feel challenged, energized—and trusted.

As we explored in Chapter 7, trust is reciprocal: "I trust you when I feel trusted." Leadership works the same way. As one Gen Z panelist told us in a ThinkLab session, "We want to provide value and feel valued by our company." When leadership is framed as sacrifice without recognition, trust breaks—and the pipeline dries up. When it's framed as mutual value, it becomes aspirational.

Idea #4: Build Purpose into the Climb

Many people think of life as two distinct stages: their work life, and what comes after. Author David Brooks describes going through each stage as akin to climbing a mountain.[13] What he calls the "first mountain" is dedicated to career and personal success, while the "second mountain" is concerned with purpose and giving back in retirement. But as Akhtar Badshah explained in our podcast episode on purpose, "There is no need to climb two mountains. Just climb one, and make sure it's not just about you."

Many Gen Zers want to rewrite that old script to Badshah's way of thinking, which benefits all of us. They don't want to postpone meaning until later. They expect their work to matter *now*.

Gamified growth answers *how* employees progress. Purpose answers *why* they stay. The two must go hand in hand: Growth that leads somewhere meaningful is what sustains engagement long-term.

Leaders can make this real by doing the following:

- **Enable self-discovery at work.** Help employees articulate their own "why," not just absorb the company's mission. (As we explored back in Chapter 3, self-reflection helps define what "better" looks like for you.)
- **Spotlight strengths.** As Badshah noted, "We spend way too much time focusing on our weaknesses. What are you good at, and how do you use it daily?"
- **Start small.** Don't wait for perfect resources—start where you are, show empathy daily, and let purpose grow. (Badshah shared how Microsoft began with a philanthropic fund of $17,000 in 1983, which grew to more than $2 billion over decades.)
- **Encourage community involvement.** Raise money for a charity, do good for the community, or gift employees a certain amount of time off each month to volunteer. In other words, build opportunities to "give back" to your for-profit organization (bringing together your first and second mountains).

Purpose isn't something to delay until you reach the second mountain. For Gen Z—and for a healthier leadership pipeline—it has to be embedded in the climb itself.

The Future of Purpose at Work

This chapter's shift comes down to a simple but powerful reframe:

FROM: Careers are cumulative.

Progress is a slow, vertical climb where years served equal steps earned. Experience is valued over experimentation, and leadership often comes with trade-offs in balance and well-being.

TO: Careers are nonlinear.

Progress is customized. Growth can be broad, deep, or fluid: Employees can choose to explore a wide range of roles in a company, gain greater expertise in one, or design their own path forward. Success is measured in skills, impact, and purpose—and the strongest leaders sustain their own well-being and that of their teams while moving across roles, projects, and even industries.

Looking Ahead: A Glimpse of 2050

If we start building jungle gyms instead of ladders now, what could the workplace look like a generation from today?

Imagine a 25-year-old charting her career not by titles but by skills. She is able to track which of her passions benefited the company and the impact she has made across disciplines. At the same time, a 55-year-old leader is still growing: taking on new assignments, experimenting with emerging tools, and demonstrating that skill development isn't constrained by age or title.

In this future, advancement doesn't drain people—it sustains them. The leadership pipeline doesn't run dry. It overflows with leaders of every generation, motivated not by endurance, but by curiosity, purpose, and the chance to build a healthier world of work.

So What? Key Takeaways from Chapter 11

This sixth shift—from ladders to jungle gyms—isn't just about career paths. It's a reset on how leadership potential is cultivated.

- **Well-being is leadership.** Advancement shouldn't demand sacrifice—it should model sustainability for both leaders and teams.
- **Progress must be visible.** Clear paths, micro-milestones, and gamified growth keep employees motivated and invested.
- **Exploration fuels innovation.** Intrapreneurship channels diverse skills and passions back into the company, turning varied interests into business value.
- **Purpose can't wait.** Meaning isn't reserved for the "second mountain" of retirement—it must be embedded in daily work at every level.

Leadership pipelines don't fill themselves. They're replenished by making growth transparent, purpose accessible, and well-being nonnegotiable.

12

Shift 7

From Meeting Overload to Meaningful Collaboration: Maximizing Synchronous and Asynchronous Time

> **The big idea:** In a world drowning in meetings, more time together doesn't necessarily equal more progress. The best teams today balance synchronous and asynchronous collaboration, using live time for group creativity and alignment, and async tools for deep thinking and follow-through.

IN ONE OF ThinkLab's research sessions with architecture and design leaders, the conversation got heated due to a surprising culprit: access to digital sources. For an industry centered around creativity, they argued, the endless scroll was stifling originality. Where leaders once traveled for inspiration, sketchbook in hand and camera at the ready, today's young talent is pulling images from Instagram and Pinterest.

The result? More sameness and less spark. As one leader summed it up: "We've solved for collaboration, but not ideation."

A few weeks later, we brought up that challenge in a follow-up ThinkLab brainstorm with Gen Z designers. Their response flipped the conversation on its head. "The issue isn't digital," one said. "Access to digital sources is good. The real issue is a time drought." She explained that she'd love to travel and immerse herself in inspiration, too. But with 80 percent of her hours billable to clients and endless meetings filling her day, Pinterest was all she had time for.

And today, her frustration echoes that of many knowledge workers outside the design field. No matter the industry, too many meetings during the day often means your "real work" spills into nights and weekends. You catch up on emails from the couch after the kids are in bed or set the alarm early just to find an hour of focus.

But it's not the digital tools that are to blame. The heart of the problem is the imbalance between group work and individual focus work. We've packed our calendars so full of back-to-back meetings that there's no oxygen left for deep reflection or fresh ideas. Collaboration is constant, but creativity is gasping for air.

The challenge is universal. Whether you're an architect, a salesperson, a manager, or another role in any industry, the issue remains: We've leaned too hard on synchronous tools, and we're starving for the time and focus space that ideation and innovation require.

Why More Meetings Haven't Led to More Progress

Before the pandemic, most of us didn't examine how—or how well—we communicated at work. In-person meetings were the default way to collaborate. Progress generally meant gathering in conference rooms or around project tables, with updates and decisions taking place in real time.

Then the world of knowledge work went fully digital overnight. Employees might have expected more freedom over their schedules since they couldn't go into the office. Instead, what emerged was fatigue. Entire calendars crammed with back-to-back Zoom calls, often with no time to grab lunch, or even use the restroom. We quickly saw that this version of work wasn't sustainable.

When offices reopened, many hoped we'd find balance. Instead, our time drought persisted. Leaders tried to recreate "togetherness" through even more collaboration in real time, but the result was clumsy: still too many calls, too much information, not enough space to think, and now a commute to boot.

Exploring a New Balance

And the data backs it up. A 2024 study found that the average employee spent 11.3 hours per week in meetings—nearly one third of their work-week.[1] But for some of you reading this, that percentage is even higher. Overall, the number of meetings has tripled since 2020, according to Microsoft.[2] All told, organizations are now spending an average of $29,000 per employee per year on meeting time alone.[3] It's a staggering investment—one that isn't necessarily translating to better outcomes.

What this revealed is greater than frustration with one too many meetings. It's a symptom of something deeper: Our communication norms haven't caught up with the reality of hybrid work. We have the technology for both synchronous and asynchronous collaboration, but we haven't yet learned how to use both with intention and balance. Until we do, communication will remain fragmented, and performance will pay the price.

What Is Synchronous vs. Asynchronous Communication?

Synchronous is communication that happens in real time. It can be in person, virtual, or hybrid, but generally means people are exchanging information in the moment with one another. Examples include phone calls, video calls, chats over lunch, and meetings where everyone is breathing the same air.

Asynchronous communication happens when there is a lag between when a message is sent and when a message is received. Examples include Slack, email, letters, short video messages, or even links to Google Docs. Generally, a message is sent when it's

(continued)

> (*continued*)
>
> convenient for one party and responded to or worked on when it's convenient for the other party.
>
> If you're in doubt as to which communication method would work best for a given message, check out "When to Choose Synchronous vs. Asynchronous Communication," posted by Australian software company Atlassian.[4]

The Imbalance at the Heart of Modern Selling

This imbalance doesn't just affect how teams think—it reshapes how entire roles operate. And in some functions, the pressure to be both constantly available and deeply thoughtful is even more pronounced. Sales is one of them.

Nowhere is this tension between synchronous and asynchronous work more evident than in sales. And in ThinkLab's research, those sellers tell us they feel the time imbalance more acutely than almost anyone—expected to be present, responsive, and relational, while also needing space to think, prepare, and create value.

As one seller explained, "I can be the seller I was in 2019—out shaking hands and kissing babies. Or the seller I was in 2021—wickedly responsive behind a screen. But I can't be both at once."

That tension mirrors the bigger challenge of modern communication: Just like meetings, selling hasn't yet found its rhythm for when to be live—and when to step back and think.

> ### Podcast Spotlight: "Sparking Creativity in a Digital World"
>
> That same theme came through powerfully in a *Design Nerds Anonymous* episode with guest expert Natalie Nixon. A creativity strategist, cited as one of the top 50 keynote speakers in the world, and author of *The Creativity Leap*, Nixon argues that time for creativity and focused work isn't a "nice to have." It's a

must-have. She defines creativity as "the ability to toggle between wonder and rigor to solve problems, generate meaning, and produce novel value."[5]

To make that balance possible, Nixon developed the "3i" framework:

- **Inquiry:** staying deeply curious by asking bold questions and surrounding yourself with people who think differently than you do
- **Improvisation:** experimenting, prototyping, and learning by building on ideas in real time
- **Intuition:** treating pattern recognition as a muscle—one that grows stronger the more we use it

But Nixon shares a strong warning about the limits of constantly optimizing your time: "The churn of work is not sustainable." Without space for deep thought and recovery, even the best tools or frameworks won't produce breakthrough ideas.

That reality resonated with leaders at CannonDesign who also took part in this episode. As Michelle Rotherham put it, "Conceptual design isn't something you can schedule into an hour and expect brilliance." And her colleague Carmen Ruiz Cruz added that in hybrid work, "everyone's always connected; you sometimes lose the focus you really need."

Their message echoes Nixon's: Creativity isn't blocked by digital tools themselves, but by the way we overload on synchronous time and starve the conditions that allow creativity to flourish.

Explore more about how to remain creative in this increasingly digital era by listening to this DNA podcast episode.

Busting a Myth: "Gen Z Is the Most Digital-Forward Generation."

That brings us to one of the biggest misconceptions about the next generation of workers.

It's easy to assume that Gen Zers—our first true digital natives—want everything fast, digital, and online. Many leaders believe synchronous meetings frustrate Gen Zers, while chat and text are their default. But ThinkLab's research shows something more complex: The pendulum is still swinging.

When asked how they prefer to reach a colleague for a quick project-related question, Gen Zers weren't all-in on digital (Figure 12.1). In fact, 41 percent of respondents chose walking over to someone's desk, making a quick call, or using other methods of synchronous communication. In other words, they prefer to communicate in real time. The other 59 percent leaned toward using Slack, Teams, or another asynchronous channel. In other words, they send communication when it's convenient and expect the other person to respond when it's convenient for them.

This split illustrates ThinkLab's "Boomer-ang Effect": Gen Zers' responses were aligned more closely to that of boomers than to millennials or Gen Xers.

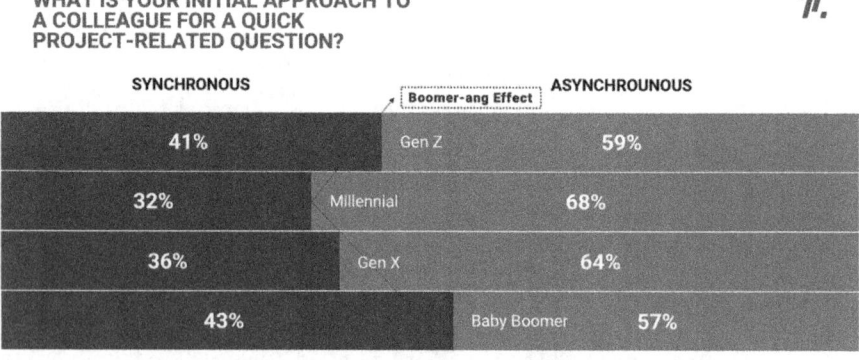

Figure 12.1 The future isn't all digital—it's balanced. Millennials skew most toward async tools, while Gen Z's preference for real-time interaction brings them more closely in line with boomers, revealing another Boomer-ang Effect.

Source: ThinkLab.design Gen Z research / with permission of ThinkLab.

Rather than racing toward a purely digital future, Gen Zers are seeking balance. They want the efficiency of asynchronous tools *and* the immediacy of live conversations. The real takeaway isn't that one mode is better than the other—it's that communication must be intentional, matching the format to the task. Synchronous communication can be more productive when aligning teams or collectively working through an issue, but asynchronous can gift each individual the time to craft a thoughtful response.

Gen Zers aren't rejecting live conversations—they're rejecting pointless ones.

How to Balance Synchronous and Asynchronous Work: Practical Ideas for Leaders and Teams

So, how do we find the balance?

Back-to-back meetings aren't the answer, but neither is a world of endless emails, Slacks, and Teams messages without any human-to-human contact. The real opportunity lies in being intentional: choosing synchronous time when energy and fast alignment are needed, and leaning on asynchronous tools when reflection, focus, and creativity matter most.

That balance doesn't happen by accident—it must be designed. Leaders and teams who master this shift will not only reclaim time and reduce fatigue, but also create the conditions for greater creativity, sharper decision-making, and more human connection.

Let's consider five ways to achieve that balance.

Idea #1: Protect Time for Deep Work

If meetings are the currency of modern work, then time for deep thinking has become the rarest commodity. As one Gen Z designer told ThinkLab, "The problem isn't that I don't want to do the work—I'll always fill the time I'm given. The problem is I'm constantly rushing, because there's so much to do. Help me put guardrails on my creative research time so I can judge the workload correctly and learn how to balance creativity with productivity."

Setting up guardrails, as this designer suggested, isn't just about avoiding burnout; it's about designing time structures that allow fresh ideas to emerge. When time for focus work is defined, deep work is prioritized, and meeting creep is checked, the quality of output rises for everyone.

Try this:

- **Set "meeting-free days."** Companies like Shopify and Asana have experimented with designating one day per week entirely free of meetings, giving teams uninterrupted time for focus and creativity.
- **Timebox for deep work.** Encourage employees to block off 90- to 120-minute sessions for heads-down tasks (a technique also known as "timeboxing," popularized by Cal Newport's book *Deep Work*). This trains teams to treat focus time as nonnegotiable.
- **Create shorter default meetings.** Change the default meeting length from 30 or 60 minutes to 25 or 50. Microsoft research showed meetings naturally expand to the time allotted, so shorter defaults save time without hurting outcomes.[6]
- **Define creative hours.** Set realistic expectations for how long specific tasks (such as research and ideation for a design project) should take so employees can plan, pace, and protect that time, whether it's 10, 20, or 100 hours.
- **Model boundaries.** Leaders should share when they block time for focus, signaling that prioritizing creativity or focus time is not only allowed but expected.

Idea #2: Redesign Meetings for a Digital-First Era

Not every conversation needs a meeting. Too often, we default to pulling people into real-time sessions that could have been handled faster, and with more clarity, asynchronously. A digital-first mindset flips the script: Share materials in advance, let people process them on their own time, and reserve synchronous moments for what truly benefits from live energy: debate, brainstorming, and decision-making.

The payoff is real. Flowtrace's analysis found managers and professionals lose 30 percent of their time in poorly designed meetings—time that could be spent on productive work.[7] According to a recent Atlassian study, 78 percent of respondents said their schedules were so overloaded with meetings that it was affecting their ability to get their work done. Similarly, 80 percent felt that cutting down on meetings would allow them to be more productive.[8] The research is clear: The key to better meetings isn't the meeting itself—it's what happens before and after. Effective prep makes your time together more insightful, and effective follow-up ensures that decisions actually turn into action.

Try this:

- **Lead with prep.** Require every invite to clearly state the goal of the meeting (such as decision-making, brainstorming, etc.). Sharing the background, context, and goals helps everyone think on their own first.
- **Consider async-first for updates.** Use tools like Teams or Slack for status reports, freeing up live time for collaboration. (Pro tip: Just make sure keeping up with these async updates doesn't take more time than just attending a meeting! Short Slack messages are easy to read, but 10 two-minute videos might as well have been a meeting.)
- **Automate follow up.** Leverage AI tools to note take, send agreed upon "to do's" after the meeting, and automate the follow up so that those items are completed before the next meeting. There are few things more frustrating in this time-starved era than meeting about the same to-do lists when nothing is actually being checked off. (For more in this, see idea 5 in this section.)

The objective: fewer meetings, better outcomes, and a culture that treats people's time and attention like the scarce resources they are.

Idea #3: Fuel Passion and Ideas

Most breakthrough ideas don't emerge in formal meetings—they are developed in the white space around them.

This isn't just theory. Here's proof that this works:

- **Google's "20% Time":** Google introduced a practice that allowed employees to devote up to one day each week—roughly 20 percent of their paid time—to projects of their own choosing.[9] The goal was to give employees autonomy to explore ideas outside their core job responsibilities. This yielded more than half of Google's flagship products, including Gmail, AdSense, Google News, and Google Maps—confirming the immense business impact of giving employees dedicated time for creativity and exploration.[10]
- **Atlassian's "20% Time":** Inspired by Google, Atlassian originally ran their own program as a six-month experiment. Employees were encouraged to spend part of their workweek on personal or innovative projects, with outcomes shared at "ShipIt" hackathons. Even when most employees used only a fraction of the time, the cultural signal was powerful, reinforcing that innovation was valued. For a variety of reasons, this program has evolved into "innovation weeks," which achieves similar results by putting that 20 percent time into a more limited "box." This means more synchronous coordination in a shorter time period.[11]
- **CannonDesign's AMP (Activate, Mobilize, Propel) program:** As Michelle Rotherham explained in our podcast episode on creativity, AMP offers another model. Designed as an internal incubator, it gives employees space and support to explore new ideas alongside their client work. Some projects evolve into new service offerings; others simply spark fresh approaches to existing challenges. Either way, the message is clear: Innovation isn't extracurricular—it's expected.

The takeaway: Curiosity isn't a side project—it's the fuel of innovation. The organizations that thrive will be those that clear calendar clutter and then channel that reclaimed time into exploring ideas. When done well, this transforms curiosity into business impact.

Idea #4: Build Rest into the Rhythm of Work

In a culture that celebrates busyness, resting is often considered a weakness. But the truth is, creativity doesn't happen when we're always "on." In our podcast episode on creativity, Natalie Nixon discusses her MTR framework (Movement, Thought, and Rest), which underscores that downtime is not wasted time. It's a core ingredient of break-through thinking. In 2025, Nixon published a book called *Move. Think. Rest.: Redefining Productivity and Our Relationship with Time*, which dives even deeper into this topic.

Hybrid work makes this even more critical. "Always on" pings, instant responses, and the blur between home and office can quietly erode focus and drain creative energy. Protecting focus means creating guardrails against constant interruptions and setting norms that respect recovery.

The companies that are taking meeting fatigue seriously are seeing tangible results. In 2023, Shopify canceled 12,000 recurring meetings involving more than three people, reclaiming an estimated 322,000 hours of employee time.[12] Their Meeting Cost Calculator pegged the potential savings at $8.4 million annually—not to mention the cultural win of "No-Meeting Wednesdays" and a new expectation that every meeting must earn its place. Shopify's COO put it simply: The change made employees more intentional with their time, freeing up energy for core tasks and projects.

Here are a few ways to build rest into the rhythm of work:

- **Normalize walking meetings.** Movement fuels thought. Encourage conversations on the go, especially for one-on-ones or check-ins.
- **Do a meeting audit.** Like Shopify, make meetings (especially reoccurring meetings) earn their keep.
- **Set boundaries on pings.** Define response-time expectations so hybrid teams don't feel tethered 24/7.
- **Flex for flow.** Allow schedules that match people's peak creative energy—whether that's morning deep work or late-night brainstorming.

■ **Model rest.** Leaders should share openly about how they recharge, making it clear that recovery happens as part of the job, not outside of it.

The takeaway: Rest isn't the absence of work—it's the fuel for better work. And as Shopify's results show, building recovery into the rhythm of work doesn't just prevent burnout—it delivers measurable business returns.

Idea #5: Leverage AI to Supercharge Asynchronous Work

And here's where AI enters the picture: It risks magnifying the busyness problem. By producing reports, summaries, and presentations more quickly than ever, AI could unintentionally flood us with more updates, more noise, more meetings unless we change our norms. Speed without intention won't save us; it will only accelerate the overload. Because AI has the potential to introduce more noise or even set productivity back, it's important to leverage it thoughtfully.

Asynchronous tools are only as powerful as the systems behind them. Too often, notes vanish after a meeting, updates get buried in chat threads, and context is lost when team members can't attend in real time. AI is changing that. By automatically capturing, organizing, and redistributing knowledge, AI allows teams to make asynchronous work both more reliable and more inclusive—without adding more administrative burden.

Microsoft's 2025 workplace collaboration data shows the difference clearly. The highest-performing teams (dubbed "Frontier Firms") organize work around flexible, async-first processes supported by AI.[13] Leaders of these teams are nearly twice as likely to say their company is thriving compared to workers globally (71 percent vs. 39 percent) and far more likely to report capacity to take on additional work (55 percent vs. 25 percent). Their secret isn't working harder; it's working smarter by letting technology do the heavy lifting of documentation and follow-through.

Try this:

- **Automate meeting capture.** Use AI to record, transcribe, and summarize meetings so those who can't attend still stay in the loop.
- **Turn notes into knowledge.** AI can tag action items, link back to past discussions, and surface decisions when you need them.
- **Build a searchable archive.** Instead of information vanishing in chat or email, AI can create living documents that preserve institutional memory.
- **Close the loop.** Use AI tools to check progress against past action items and nudge the tasks' owners, ensuring follow-up doesn't fall through the cracks.

The takeaway: Leveraging AI ensures that follow through is completed freeing humans to focus on higher-value work.

The Future of Collaboration

This comes down to a fundamental mindset shift.

FROM: Synchronous meetings are markers of progress.

Communication is centered on synchronous time. Gathering in person (or on video) is the default for updates, decision-making, and proof of productivity.

TO: Progress stems from a balanced blend of synchronous and asynchronous communication.

Synchronous time is reserved for creative energy, trust-building, and making critical decisions. Asynchronous tools (and, increasingly, AI) handle updates, documentation, and follow-through, making communication more efficient.

Looking Ahead: A Glimpse of 2050

If we follow this path, what might the workplace of the future look like?

Imagine logging in on Monday morning and, instead of facing a wall of back-to-back meetings, you find a concise digital brief: every update you need, summarized and tagged by AI. Better yet, this report is delivered to you via a 10-minute podcast, filling only a portion of your commute as you walk, drive, or scooter to your work location for the day. This ensures you're in the know but leaves your brain open for a mental break before you start your day and your calendar open focused work and purposeful human-to-human connection and collaboration throughout your day.

When it's time to meet live, the agenda is clear, everyone is bringing thoughtful contributions due to their individual prep time, and all are ready to work together. Afterward, AI-generated notes and action items circulate automatically, linking back to past decisions and nudging owners on next steps—so no idea is lost, and no one is left out.

In this vision of the future, meetings aren't the metric of progress—outcomes are. And by treating how we collaborate as a choice, not a default, organizations can reclaim time, fuel creativity, and make every interaction—whether async or live—more human and more valuable.

So What? Key Takeaways from Chapter 12

This shift—from "more meetings" to intentional collaboration—isn't just about convenience. It's about designing time to fuel productivity, creativity, and connection in a hybrid, AI-driven world.

- **More isn't necessarily better.** The number of meetings has tripled since 2020, but outcomes haven't improved. Progress is measured in results, not in hours spent together.
- **Prep and follow-up make the meeting.** The value of live time comes from what happens before (setting a clear purpose, sharing context) and after (follow-through, holding owners accountable).
- **Cut to create.** Eliminating low-value meetings frees up space for deep work, curiosity, and innovation: the factors that actually drive business forward.
- **Rest is fuel, not a perk.** Downtime and white space are essential for creativity and sustainable performance.
- **AI makes async smarter.** Top-performing teams use AI to capture notes, tag action items, and build searchable archives, so information flows without requiring everyone to be "in the room."
- **Balance is the goal.** Synchronous and asynchronous aren't competing modes—they're complementary. The leaders who thrive will be the ones who balance both.

13

Shift 8

From Messenger to Multiplier: How to Communicate to Expand Your Impact

> **The big idea:** In a world of bigger teams, shorter attention spans, and fewer chances to be in the room, the leaders who win aren't saying more—they're saying it clearer. The best communication today is bite-sized, shareable, and designed to travel without you.

WHEN I LAUNCHED ThinkLab, writing became my primary vehicle for sharing research. Those 1,200-word articles were how I built credibility and visibility: from my early blogging days for *The Huffington Post* to later features in *Interior Design, Metropolis,* and now viral pieces in *Forbes* and *MIT Sloan Management Review.* Long-form writing was my superpower. But when I tried to translate those skills into short-form video, my efforts fell flat.

For example, like many of us, I'd take a polite beat before launching into my script. (If you've spent time on social media, you've probably seen Gen Z mock this habit as the "millennial pause." For a good laugh, check out TikTok's @mikehege.realtor, where a Gen Z employee who was supposed to be editing his videos for social media compiled nothing but clips of his repeated pre-speech breaths.[1])

The problem? Today every extra word or pause risks losing your audience before you've made your point. Users on Facebook spend an average of just 1.7 seconds viewing a piece of content on mobile before deciding whether to engage or scroll past.[2] And the same reality applies beyond social media. Professor Gloria Mark at the University of California, Irvine, found that the average attention span for knowledge workers has dropped from 2.5 minutes in 2004 to around 44 seconds in 2021.[3] We all have less time than ever. So, whether online or at work, if you want your message to land and to have the widest reach, you have to lead with what matters most.

I learned this lesson the hard way through my first experiments with short-form video. In my generation (Gen X), it was polite to start every conversation by introducing yourself. Naturally, I brought that same instinct online—and it didn't work. Gen Z is showing us why. They've grown up on digital-first platforms where attention is earned in seconds, not minutes. An introduction doesn't stop the scroll; a hook does. Social media has flipped the script: lead with the punchline first, then let your audience decide whether to scroll, click, or dive deeper.

That's where the communication pyramid comes in (Figure 13.1). The structure that works best looks like this:

- **The Hook (Why it matters to you):** Grab attention first. Give away the one thing you really want them to know.
  For example: "What Gen Z is asking for isn't all that different than what the rest of us want."
- **Credibility (Why trust me):** Share why you are a credible source for this information.
  For me: "I've spent over 500 hours studying Gen Z."
- **Proof (What you need to know):** Keep it to three points; the brain can't remember more. Think concise, quotable, actionable.
- **Call to action (What to do next):** This directs your viewer or reader to where they can find more information, dig deeper, or take the next step.
  For example: "Click here to listen to this podcast."

THE NEW COMMUNICATION PYRAMID

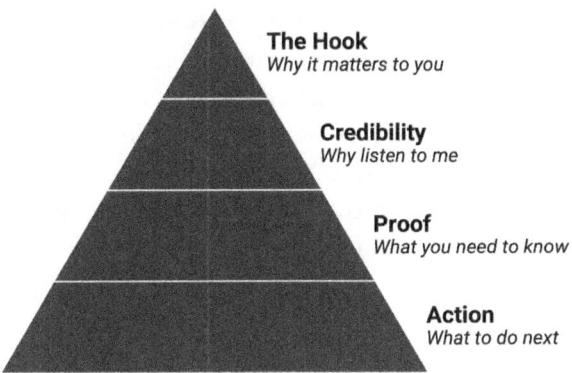

The Hook
Why it matters to you

Credibility
Why listen to me

Proof
What you need to know

Action
What to do next

Figure 13.1   In an age of shrinking attention spans, clarity beats complexity. The New Communication Pyramid flips the script—starting with why it matters, then building trust, proof, and action in just four simple steps.

This model feels counterintuitive because it flips how most of us were taught to communicate. Traditional communication is linear: first, the setup, then the context, then the conclusion. But in today's workplace, that structure misses the mark: people tune out before you ever get to your point.

This layered approach meets people where they are—using short-form content to capture attention, then offering deeper paths for those ready to engage further. I've even used this approach for the ideas that anchor this book. I first explored these concepts with a 12-minute TEDx talk. The video was picked up by TED.com and within a few months got half a million views, proving how this type of short-form content can help reach a wide audience, quickly. For those who'd like to know more, there's social media content (the talk has also been featured on the podcast *TED Talks Daily,* for example). Now, for those ready for a deeper dive into data, proof points, and what to do as a result: this book. And for teams that want to go a step further, ThinkLab offers keynotes to share direct application of these concepts.

Expanding Your Reach in B2B Sales

Nowhere has this shift from messenger to multiplier shown up more clearly in ThinkLab's research than with business-to-business (B2B) sellers. Measuring the effectiveness of internal communication is notoriously difficult, but sales interactions provide a front-row view of what's working—and what isn't as measured by revenue.

Forrester reports that across industries, the average B2B decision-making team has grown from as few as 2 to as many as 13 people.[4] In today's economic environment—marked by rising costs and heightened risk aversion—it's no surprise that project cycles are slowing down.

ThinkLab's research into the built environment shows the same trend. In a series of live research events throughout 2024 and 2025, we convened stakeholders with decision-making power over designing offices, hospitals, schools, and hotels. On average, we learned, the decision-making committees for such projects have doubled in size over the past five years.[5] Committees have swelled as companies pull in more voices—driven by inflation, risk aversion, and the ease of joining via Zoom. At the same time, the average sales rep's face time with these important decision-makers has been cut in half.

The math is brutal: twice the number of decision-makers, half the access. Which means communication has to do more heavy lifting than ever. It has to be clearer, more succinct, more powerful, and above all, more shareable because those reps aren't always *in the room*. With half the face time and twice the people, today's B2B rep must equip others to carry the message forward—quickly, clearly, and with confidence. You scale your impact as a salesperson not by talking more, but by making ideas easy to repeat, forward, and champion when you're not in the room. The most successful reps today are those who can scale their time and amplify their impact through others carrying that message forward without you.

And the same is true inside organizations. It's not enough to strip your message down to fewer words. The goal is to spark action when you're not in the room. And this is not just a key skill for leaders. Whether you're presenting to executives, pitching an idea to peers, or updating your manager, the same rule applies: Make the "why it matters" so clear and compelling that others can't help but share it.

That's the shift Gen Z has forced us to see communication that is easy to understand, easy to pass along, and powerful enough to cut through the noise. Because in today's workplace, no one has time for anything—but everyone makes time for what's clear and relevant.

One theme surfaced repeatedly in our live discussions with key decision-makers: the growing need to "manage up."

As one real estate executive explained, "I grew up in this industry. Many of my superiors did not. But today, they are involved in the decisions. That means I spend an exorbitant amount of my time simplifying and reframing the information outside partners give me so that my bosses can understand it and help get to a decision."

Podcast Spotlight: "Managing Up: Today's Crucial Skill You Weren't Taught"

In this *Design Nerds Anonymous* episode, we turned to Dr. J.J. Peterson of StoryBrand to unpack how to communicate with more clarity and impact and even "manage up" when it feels we have more bosses than ever. StoryBrand is best known for helping organizations simplify their marketing messages, but we find its framework is just as powerful for everyday workplace communication.

"Every time we process information, our brains burn calories. And because our brains want to conserve energy, they tune out anything confusing or irrelevant," Dr. Peterson explained. "If your message isn't clear, people won't just misunderstand it—they'll ignore it."[6]

Here's how to clarify your message:

- **Lead with the problem.** Don't start with what you want. Start with the challenge your audience is already facing—so they nod along and stay engaged.
- **Position them as the hero.** Your role is the guide: Show empathy, offer a clear plan, and provide evidence that builds trust.
- **End with stakes.** Make it clear what's gained if they act—or lost if they don't.

(continued)

(continued)

When you frame communication this way, you lower the brain's "calorie burn" and make it effortless for others to carry your message into the next room, the next meeting, or the next level of leadership.

Discover more about how the StoryBrand marketing approach can actually help you communicate better at work by listening to this DNA podcast.

The Medium Matters as Much as the Message

However, even the clearest message can miss its target if it's delivered in the wrong format. Today, we have more choices in how a message is delivered than ever: talking, texting, emailing, messaging on Slack, videos, and the list goes on. And it may not surprise you that different generations naturally gravitate to different approaches.

Our research shows that, for quick project questions, Gen Z overwhelmingly prefers communicating on chat platforms such as Slack or Teams (49 percent) or simply walking over to a desk for an in-person chat (36 percent). As for email? Just 9 percent of both millennials and Gen Zers prefer it. Compare that to baby boomers, 27 percent of whom still default to email. (Note: Did you spot the "Boomer-ang effect" in Figure 13.2? Gen Zers are more aligned with baby boomers when it comes to walking over to speak to a colleague, compared with millennials or Gen Xers.)

Each generation has its own preferences for approaching colleagues, and that fact highlights an important truth. It's not enough to

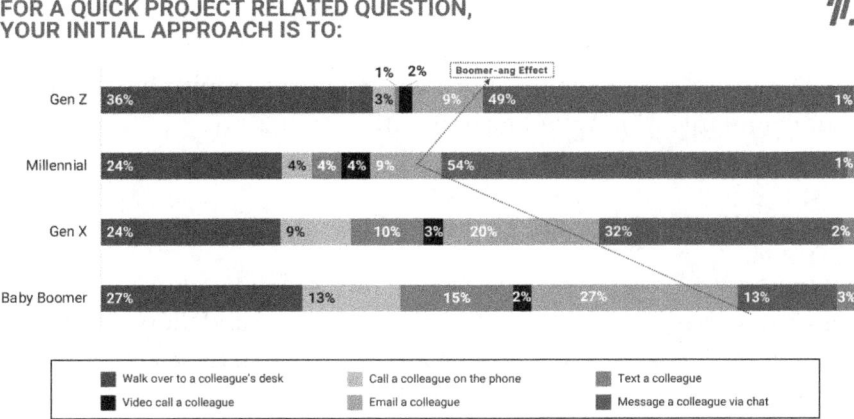

FOR A QUICK PROJECT RELATED QUESTION, YOUR INITIAL APPROACH IS TO:

Figure 13.2 Communication styles are shifting—but not in a straight line. Gen Z blends digital chat with real-time conversation, looping back toward boomers' preference for direct connection and revealing another Boomer-ang Effect in action. Email, once the universal default, now ranks lowest among younger generations.

craft the right message—you also have to choose the right container. And the burden sits with the creator of the message. The best communicators are intentional about how their message will land: a quick Slack when speed matters, a one-page summary instead of a 20-slide deck for executives, or a face-to-face conversation when nuance and trust are critical.

Communicating for Impact: Practical Ideas for Leaders and Teams

Considering that attention spans are shrinking and project committees are growing, communication isn't just a soft skill—it's a modern work survival skill. The old approaches simply can't keep up with today's pace.

The good news? Gen Z is showing us what works. This generation—raised on short-form content and constant streams of information—has forced us all to sharpen a digital-first approach to communication. They remind us that in a world of endless inputs, people only make time for what is clear, relevant, and easy to pass along.

And while the following ideas are shaped by next-gen expectations, they're not just for Gen Z. The skills of making messages clearer, more shareable, and easier to act on are useful for everyone—because no one has time for confusion anymore.

Here are three ways to shift from messenger to multiplier and make your communication travel farther with less friction.

Idea #1: Build Universal Business Fluency

No matter your role, today's workplace demands a baseline understanding of how business works. Why? Because the foundation of effective communication is relevance. A message only sticks if the recipient understands how it impacts their business, their role, or their goals. Too often, great ideas stall not because they lack merit, but because the person presenting them can't connect the dots to business cost, risk, or outcomes.

And let's be honest: While we all want fulfilling work and purpose, we also need to work to make money—and we only have jobs if the companies we work for can make money. That's why communication has to link every idea back to business fundamentals.

The research backs this up. FINRA's 2025 study on financial capability found that fewer than one-third of U.S. adults could correctly answer basic financial literacy questions about interest rates and inflation.[7] And while you may assume it's the youngest among us who struggle with business fluency, this isn't just a blind spot for Gen Z. These knowledge gaps persist across every generation. The conclusion: Financial literacy isn't just about money. It's about confidence in decision-making, the ability to evaluate trade-offs, and the skill to communicate why an idea matters in business terms. In today's larger, more complex committees, that fluency is table stakes.

Try this:

- **Teach business basics.** Build financial and business literacy into training for all employees, not just executives. It equips everyone to explain ideas in the language decision-makers understand.
- **Focus on outcomes.** Encourage employees of all roles to pitch ideas in terms of ROI, risk reduction, or alignment with organizational priorities.

- **Coach the "So what?"** Before presenting, ask: "Why should this matter to the business?" If the link isn't clear, refine until it is. Remember: Sustainable success comes from aligning business goals with human ones.
- **Model it.** Leaders can reinforce this habit by explaining not just *what* decision was made, but *why*—showing the direct tie to strategy, cost, or impact.

The takeaway: For your ideas to have the greatest impact, make it clear how they can help the team meet its collective business goals.

Idea #2: Lead with the Headline, Then Layer in the Story

Marketing has already proven this works. For example, StoryBrand, mentioned in the podcast interview earlier in this chapter, has helped organizations from Farmers Insurance to Hilton Hotels sharpen their messaging—and in every case, the payoff was growth, loyalty, or sales. Their principle is simple: Clear, concise communication wins.

If that clarity can attract millions of customers, it can also move colleagues and decision-makers. Internally, the same skills apply: Start with the headline, then layer context for those who want more.

And in practice? This might look like:

- **A catchy subject line that makes an email worth opening:** If your audience only remembers one thing, what should it be? "Three fixes to cut project delays in half" works better than "Project updates."
- **A slide title that sums up the takeaway:** "This option saves $2M over three years" is better than "Financial model scenario 2."
- **A repeatable phrase that sticks in people's heads:** Test whether someone could forward your email, repeat your phrase, or read your slide title and get the essence without you in the room. For example: A recent ThinkLab AI workshop with product manufacturers obsessively used the phrase "human in the loop" to emphasize that AI should augment, not replace, humans. That phrase was easy to remember and share.

Speaking of AI, the rise of AI makes this shift even more attainable. Input your headline and proof points into AI tools to generate concise summaries, sharper subject lines, or repeatable phrases. (The caveat: AI can accelerate clarity, but only if you feed it the right structure. Garbage in, garbage out still applies.)

The takeaway: Attention is earned, not given. The leaders who start with the headline—and use today's tools to make their message simple enough to repeat—are the ones whose ideas will travel the farthest.

Idea #3: Customize Your Communication

You can't tailor every message to every preference—that's impossible, especially on multigenerational teams. The goal is balance. Digital tools extend reach and speed. Human interactions build depth and trust. The most effective communicators blend the two.

The goal isn't perfection. It's making your message easy to absorb, easy to pass along, and easy to revisit—no matter who encounters it.

Try this:

- **Default to chat for speed.** Quick internal nudges on Slack or Teams often get faster responses than long emails.
- **Send a short video recap.** A 90-second short-form video captures tone and intent in ways text can't.
- **Write emails for forwarding.** Assume they'll be shared upward. Put the key takeaway in the first three sentences, with bullets for clarity.
- **Format for the audience.** Execs want top-line clarity, peers may need context, and juniors may need detail. Adjust the medium accordingly.
- **Make space for human moments.** Deliver sensitive feedback, complex negotiations, or relationship-building conversations face-to-face or live.
- **Use AI as a format shifter.** Create long drafts if needed, then let AI condense them into a chat snippet, bullet summary, or script for video.

The new rule is simple: Clarity isn't just about the *what*. It's also about the *how*.

The Future of Communication

The essence of this shift is a new lens.

FROM: Communication is top-down and analog-first.

- Leaders act as messengers, filtering information and deciding what teams need to know.
- Messages are delivered in long form: memos, meetings, and detailed updates that expect full attention up front.
- Communication defaults to analog-first, with digital tools seen as add-ons rather than primary channels.

TO: Communication is customized and scalable.

- The best leaders act as multipliers, making information clear, concise, and easy to share.
- Messages are crafted in layers: bite-sized at the top to capture attention, with detail available for those who want to go deeper.
- Digital and human communication are blended intentionally and authentically: digital for the sake of reach and speed, human for depth and trust.

Looking Ahead: A Glimpse of 2050

If we follow this path, what might 2050 look like?

Imagine a workplace where communication travels as far and fast as the best ideas deserve—without distortion, friction, or wasted time.

AI will play a central role in that future. Instead of long email chains or meetings packed with status updates, AI assistants could instantly condense information into tailored formats: a 20-second video recap for executives, a visual snippet for peers, and detailed notes for those who need depth. Messages could scale naturally across platforms, carrying the same clarity whether whispered in a hallway, forwarded to a client, or dropped into a global team chat.

But here's the key: At the time of writing, many still fear AI. And those fears aren't unfounded. Speed without judgment risks flooding us with noise instead of delivering clarity. That's why the human role will matter more, not less. While AI can make us faster, it's the human capacity for empathy, perspective-taking, and human-to-human connection that ensures communication lands and inspires action. The leaders who thrive will be those who pair AI efficiency with human nuance—the ability to read a room, sense what's unsaid, and tailor messages with emotional intelligence.

In this version of the future, influence isn't measured by who talks the most or who controls the meeting. It's measured by whose ideas travel farthest—and with the most impact. Gen Z's demand for brevity, clarity, and digital-first connection could be the spark that pushes all of us toward a more efficient, inclusive, and human way of communicating—if we choose to act on it.

So What? Key Takeaways from Chapter 13

This shift—from messenger to multiplier—isn't just a Gen Z expectation. It's a signal that in a world of bigger project teams, shrinking attention spans, less face time, and more connections across geographies, the way we communicate must evolve—faster, clearer, and with more intention—so ideas can travel farther with greater impact.

- **Clarity is currency.** The best messages are clear, concise, and crafted to stick—so they can be carried forward without you in the room.
- **Start with the headline.** Lead with the one thing you want remembered. Let people choose whether to dive deeper into context and detail.
- **Match message to medium.** Use chat for speed, video for nuance, email for recordkeeping, and face-to-face for trust. Blending digital and human intentionally makes communication scale.
- **Make it repeatable.** A message that can't be forwarded, summarized, or retold isn't a multiplier. The real test: Can someone else share it accurately in three sentences or less?
- **Equip your champions.** Whether it's a client advocate or a manager pitching your idea upstream, give them the crisp bullets or one-liner they need to succeed.
- **AI is an amplifier, not a replacement.** Use it to streamline formats, draft summaries, or sharpen phrasing—but keep humans in the loop for empathy, nuance, and trust.

14

Shift 9

From Apprenticeship to Accessibility: Mentorship for Every Generation

> **The big idea:** Today's strongest cultures don't rely on osmosis for mentorship—they make guidance accessible. By blending digital tools with human connection, leaders can reimagine mentorship to flow across generations, extend beyond company walls, and strengthen careers at every stage.

IN ONE OF ThinkLab's sessions with our Gen Z Cohort, a Gen Z participant anonymously shared a major frustration with return-to-work policies: "We are told we have to come into the office because of mentorship, but when I get there, I'm just on Zoom in a different place. I'm not getting more because I am sitting here. We have to get more intentional about why I am here."

This frustration captures one of the biggest cracks in today's workplace logic. For decades, mentorship was mostly informal, even invisible at times. Even in formalized programs ("Here's your mentor!"), the real learning often happened through osmosis: by listening in on meetings, shadowing superiors, overhearing hallway conversations, watching how leaders handled challenges.

But this apprenticeship model works only when careers unfold solely in physical space: one company, one office, one predictable path. This system made sense in its time. (After all, before Zoom, Google, YouTube, or AI, the only way to learn was to sit near someone more experienced.) But today's workforce looks very different: hybrid schedules, quicker role changes, and careers that span numerous companies and industries. Even so, after decades of refining the apprenticeship model, it's no surprise many leaders still default to thinking of face-to-face as the only "real" form of mentorship.

In other words, as ThinkLab research participant Isabel Das put it in a *Design Nerds Anonymous* podcast episode: "The traditional workplace is set up to only do that mentorship, and that culture building, in person." Das added, "So, until the way we work and the way we build culture in our offices can be translated to a [digital-first] environment, there is that need and that push for younger generations to go into the office."[1]

Translation: Until we reframe our mentorship models for the world we are living in, the office remains the default setting for mentorship— but the problem remains. As another cohort participant noted, "Mentorship doesn't always come successfully just because you're in person."

And leaders are feeling the strain, too. A seasoned leader from a prominent design firm shared in another ThinkLab session: "I used to spend 25 percent of my time mentoring. Now, it's over a third." With workloads already stretched across projects and time zones, even well-intentioned mentors risk burnout.

Gen Zers, however, aren't turning down mentorship. They're just saying the old playbook doesn't work like it used to. What they're asking for instead is an evolution: clearer guidance, more inclusive access, and a shift from proximity-based osmosis to intentional, flexible systems of support.

The Mentorship Myths Holding Us Back

Mentorship may be one of the most overused arguments in support of returning to the office. But scratch beneath the surface, and you'll find the story is far more complicated. Many of the assumptions leaders cling to about how mentorship works are rooted in an older model that simply doesn't fit today's workplace. The truth? Some of our most deeply held beliefs about who mentors whom, where mentorship happens, and what the next generation actually wants are due for a serious rethink. Let's unpack those myths:

Myth #1: Mentorship Only Works If You're in the Office

In today's increasingly digital, globally interconnected world, mentorship isn't limited to face-to-face, especially for Gen Z. In a recent cohort session, we asked our Gen Zers to name a mentor who supported them or to share a situation where a mentor was helpful to them. About half of the stories described face-to-face interactions, but the other half took place virtually. Fluidity between the digital and physical world is so deeply ingrained, Gen Zers don't differentiate between the two. For them, it is natural for mentorship to occur in digital spaces: from shadowing a leader on Zoom, being invited into a client call virtually, or even being acknowledged in a chat thread.

The lesson? Mentorship isn't disappearing—it's expanding. To be effective today, we must blend formats: using in-person moments for depth, nuance, and relationship-building, while leaning on digital tools to broaden access and visibility.

Myth #2: Only Seasoned Employees Can Be Mentors

Today's workforce is showing us that mentorship must evolve. Gen Z often finds formal programs stiff or forced—and many prefer learning from peers just a step ahead.

As one cohort participant explained, "A lot of times, it feels awkward if someone is just assigned as your mentor. You don't always click, and then it feels forced." Another added that when mentorship is overly formalized, it can feel more like checking a box than helping you grow. By contrast, what can often resonate more is guidance from those just slightly further along: "Sometimes I learn the most from somebody just a year or two ahead of me, because they remember what it's like to be in my shoes."

In our research, we were surprised to discover how early in their career this generation of Gen Zers already see themselves as mentors. As one cohort participant explained, "I already mentor people on my team just because I'm the one who's been here longer." Others described guiding interns, helping newer teammates, or supporting peers just a step behind them. For this generation, mentoring less-experienced colleagues isn't reserved for senior leaders—it's simply a natural, reciprocal part of how work gets done.

Gen Z employees are also flipping the apprenticeship model on its head. While *reverse mentorship*—younger workers sharing knowledge with more senior colleagues—isn't new, its value has never been greater given the pace of change in the workplace. The challenge is twofold: retaining next-gen talent *and* preserving the vast tacit knowledge that organizations are losing as Baby Boomers retire. According to leadership scholar Jennifer Jordan of the Institute for Management Development, employees who participate in reverse mentorship programs are about 30 percent more likely to stay with their company than non-paired peers who don't.[2]

At the same time, we can do more to help senior leaders share their experience in ways that connect across generations. Many seasoned professionals hold decades of insights that remain highly relevant, but the ways we exchange information have evolved. By creating space, tools, and structures for them to pass on that knowledge—whether through new formats, storytelling platforms, or collaborative learning—we ensure their wisdom continues to shape the future. This isn't about replacing old methods with new ones; it's about combining them so that institutional knowledge becomes a living, shared resource.

ThinkLab research has found that a significant portion of the workforce is still in search of quality mentorship. Surprisingly, it's Gen X—not Gen Z—who most want a mentor and yet don't have one, showing that the hunger for guidance spans generations (Figure 14.1).

The lesson is clear: Mentorship isn't a one-way street anymore. The most resilient organizations will treat mentorship as a multidirectional exchange, where wisdom flows across levels, functions, and generations. Done well, this not only engages Gen Z, but also satisfies the wider workforce's growing appetite for guidance and connection.

Myth #3: Reverse Mentorship Is Only About Teaching Digital Tools

When people think of reverse mentoring, their minds may naturally go to a Gen Z employee showing a senior manager how to make a TikTok video or master the newest software. But the real value goes beyond these technical tutorials. Gen Z is fluent in the subtle "digital body language" of today's online communication—knowing intuitively how long a message should be, when a thumbs-up emoji feels casual versus dismissive, and why starting a text with "Dear Amanda" never lands.

HOW WOULD YOU DESCRIBE YOUR CURRENT MENTORSHIP SITUATION?

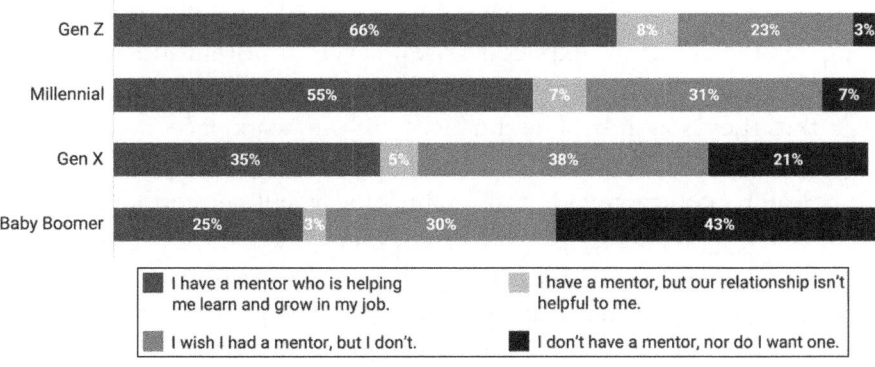

| | I have a mentor who is helping me learn and grow in my job. | I have a mentor, but our relationship isn't helpful to me. |
| I wish I had a mentor, but I don't. | I don't have a mentor, nor do I want one. |

NOTE: SOME CHARTS DO NOT SUM TO 100% DUE TO ROUNDING.

Figure 14.1 ThinkLab research reveals that the desire for mentorship spans generations. In fact, Gen X—not Gen Z—is the group most likely to want a mentor yet not have one.

For older generations, raised in an analog-first world, sometimes these subtleties don't come naturally. One senior participant in ThinkLab's research sessions said, "I'd love for Gen Z to help me learn software tools, but beyond that, there are digital nuances I don't naturally pick up on." Yet these nuances now have an incredible impact on influence and trust in the modern workplace. At best, reverse mentorship isn't about technical shortcuts—it's about learning the soft skills of clarity, tone, and connection in a digital-first workplace.

And if you don't have a Gen Z mentor handy, Erica Dhawan's book *Digital Body Language* is a great place to start. Dhawan explains how to choose emojis, punctuation, and even your channel of communication, among other things, and she demonstrates how these are all part of a vital set of skills worth learning consciously.

Myth #4: Gen Z Never Wants to Ask for Help

Here's a story I often tell: My kids would rather learn to tie their shoes from YouTube than from their dad. Why? Because on YouTube they can pause, rewind, replay, and do it again until they've mastered it. Their dad—an Army Ranger—was not built with those same functions (as you can imagine!).

That same instinct shows up for Gen Zers at work. They have grown up in a world where it feels like everything is Googleable: how to fix a faucet, learn a spreadsheet formula, troubleshoot a code bug. Naturally, they expect to "self-serve" information whenever possible.

But there's a rub: The nuances of the workplace don't always Google well.

Search "contract-grade task chair," and you'll get consumer results that don't apply. Look up "how to tell a coworker they're wrong," and you'll find advice of questionable quality. In any industry, the problem is the same: Google can't teach you how *your* company handles procurement approvals, navigating internal politics, or how to interpret the nuances of your industry in a client request for proposal (RFP).

That's why, in our research, Gen Z told us the same thing again and again: "Help me self-serve the easy stuff, and give me a safe, direct line to a human for the hard stuff." Gen Zers don't lack the initiative or desire to learn—they often just don't know where to start. And that's not unique to Gen Z. It's the same challenge every previous generation has faced early in their careers. What's different for this generation is that, in nearly every other area of their lives outside of work, Gen Zers can use digital tools to find a solution. And they feel that going online to find answers is often less embarrassing than asking someone.

Some organizations are already adapting to this mindset. One design firm in our research created a searchable library of short technical videos to answer repeat questions from junior designers on the interior design project process. Another industry-wide tool called The Design POP has turned webinars into a library of two-minute clips, so designers who work at furniture dealers can instantly find the snippet they need without watching a long-winded webinar. I am sure the nuances of your industry could lend themselves to similar approaches: Sales teams at your company could clip two-minute CRM how-tos, while finance creates "how we close the books here" micro-videos, and product teams keep a searchable glossary of internal acronyms.

But digital can't do it all. When situations get messy or political, employees still need a human to address their questions. Yet the barriers are real: 39 percent of Gen Z employees say they hesitate to ask for help because they don't want to bother their manager, and another 22 percent fear looking stupid (Figure 14.2). Unlike everything else in their lives, this is the one area they can't just Google.

That's where leaders come in. The key isn't having all the answers—it's making it feel safe to ask questions. In this new-to-all-of-us, digital-first workplace, we can't assume the norms are obvious. What feels intuitive to seasoned professionals often feels unclear to those just starting out. If only 11 percent of Gen Zers "always" ask for help when they need it, as our research has found, it's on leaders to help set ground rules—and then follow through. That might mean holding "office hours" on Slack (where many feel more comfortable asking for support) or using face-to-face one-on-ones to coach which questions are best resolved in person versus what can be solved digitally. (For example, if there's been 22 emails on the topic, it may be best to just walk over to that coworker's desk or pick up the phone!) Once expectations are stated out loud, asking gets easier—and mentoring becomes possible.

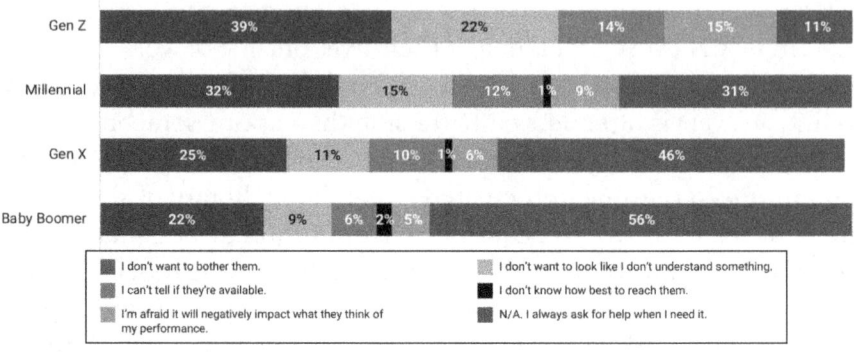

NOTE: SOME CHARTS DO NOT SUM TO 100% DUE TO ROUNDING.

Figure 14.2   For many next-gen employees, it's not a lack of curiosity that holds them back—it's fear. Most hesitate to ask for help because they don't want to interrupt or look unprepared.

The formula is simple, but powerful: Self-serve the easy stuff, direct-connect for the hard stuff. Digital tools scale efficiency, but figuring out *how* to form that human connection builds confidence, creating a mentorship model that's both sustainable and effective.

Better Mentorship for Every Generation: Practical Ideas for Leaders and Teams

If the old rules of mentorship are breaking down, that's not just an issue for Gen Z—it's an issue for the workplace as a whole. The good news? Gen Z is pushing us to evolve—and their expectations may be exactly what every generation needs to succeed as we transition mentorship from only IRL (in real life) to a phygital version. This cohort grew up with on-demand learning, fluid networks, and digital-first communication. They want guidance, but in ways that are flexible, inclusive, and fit the realities of modern work.

And while the following ideas are sparked by a next-gen perspective, they aren't just for Gen Z. The truth is, employees at every stage—from Gen X leaders who quietly crave mentorship to millennials navigating mid-career pivots—benefit when we broaden, diversify, and modernize how mentorship happens.

Next we'll look at three ways to shift from outdated models to more dynamic, future-ready approaches to mentorship.

Idea #1: Make Mentorship Less "Cringe." (That's Gen Z for "Awkward")

One of the biggest complaints we hear from Gen Z is that formal mentorship programs often feel "forced." When the chemistry isn't there, the relationship rarely sticks. And when mentors don't follow through—because they're too busy or distracted—it makes the experience even more frustrating.

The fix isn't to abandon mentorship, but to rethink the format. Instead of rigid pairings that rely only on IRL connections, create lighter, opt-in structures—with digital options when appropriate—that make mentorship feel natural rather than obligatory. Think "buddy systems" that match peers just a step or two ahead, short-term pairings based around a project, or rotational programs where people can try multiple mentors (with easy off-ramps if it's not working). These approaches not only reduce pressure but also make it easier for busy senior leaders to commit, because the time frame is clear and finite.

For example, at SANDOW Design Group, we piloted a program called Together, a digital platform where both mentors and mentees apply and define their goals. Participants are matched, then given a six-week series of structured sessions—complete with agendas, pre-work, and follow-up metrics. I personally had two matches that created lasting internal connections (and one that wasn't a fit, which the program's built-in "outs" made easy to exit). The best part? The two-way design. As a senior team member, sometimes I shared something with my matches I knew they'd find useful, but other times I asked for advice.

These approaches reduce pressure, create more authentic connections, and help normalize mentorship as a positive habit, not an obligation. As one participant explained: "It's easier when you make it feel more like a buddy than a boss. It takes away the nerves and makes the experience positive."

Idea #2: Think Beyond Your Walls

For too long, mentorship has been defined as an internal exchange. But careers no longer progress in one place. People move across organizations, industries, and even geographies more than ever. If mentorship is tied only to a single company, it risks being too narrow, too fragile, and too transactional. Today, mobility and external networks carry just as much weight in shaping careers and reputations.

And the workforce itself is shifting. From 2024 to 2034, the fastest-growing age groups in the U.S. workforce will be employees 75 and older (rising by 69 percent) and those aged 65 to 74 (rising by 15 percent), according to the Bureau of Labor Statistics.[3] Major labor reports and economic analyses attribute this trend to longer life expectancy, financial necessity, and demand for expertise. The members of these age groups are also often working on their own terms in consulting roles, part-time employment, and other flexible arrangements. With more generations working side by side than ever before, expanding mentorship beyond company walls isn't just a perk. It's a necessity.

That's why the most effective mentorship model now spans boundaries. It connects employees to outside voices, broader networks, and diverse perspectives that can't always be found in one organization. And here's the business case: When your people gain fresh input from beyond your walls, they bring that knowledge back, making your teams more innovative, more resilient, and more connected to the wider marketplace. Just as importantly, it builds your reputation as a company that develops people for long-term career success, whether they stay with you for two years or twenty.

Podcast Spotlight: "Is Mentorship Dead?"

This episode of *Design Nerds Anonymous* examines how mentorship can evolve into broader, transformational relationships that help people grow—and help organizations thrive—long after a single role or employer. "I think it's time to rethink career development," noted episode guest Dost Bardouille, director of sustainability at Swinerton. "The traditional approaches are foundational and necessary, but they're not enough anymore."[4]

Here's how new approaches build on—but also differ from—traditional mentorship:

- **Mentorship** builds technical and tactical skills and often stops at the walls of one company.
- **Sponsorship** goes further: Leaders put their social capital on the line to advocate for their mentees' advancement.
- **Championship** expands beyond the confines of one company. Leaders champion talent across an entire industry, creating opportunities that move careers forward while also driving diversity, equity, and inclusion.

By widening the lens beyond mentorship alone, organizations don't just support individual growth—they future-proof themselves. The companies that embrace sponsorship and championship create deeper networks of trust, stronger pipelines of diverse talent, and more resilient cultures that can thrive no matter where people's careers take them next.

Learn more about modern approaches to mentorship by listening to this episode of the DNA podcast.

Idea #3: Share the Mentorship Load

Leaders admit, "It's harder to teach the things we don't even realize we know," and the informal coaching that used to happen in shared spaces is harder to replicate in hybrid or remote settings. At the same time, managers are stretched thinner than ever.

Rather than assuming managers alone should carry the mentorship load, organizations can create systems that spread it out:

- Make space for peer-driven mentorship.
- Embrace external voices through championship and sponsorship.
- Put in place cross-functional "task forces" to identify more comprehensive ways to fill any major gaps with both seniors and junior staff.

Think of it like a modern chore chart: Clearly define the areas where guidance is needed, then identify who is best equipped to cover them. Sometimes, it's a senior leader. Sometimes, it's a peer who just solved the same problem last week. Sometimes, it's someone outside the company who brings fresh perspective.

When organizations take this approach, they accomplish two things at once: They give young professionals a springboard to solve business challenges themselves, and they reduce the risk of manager burnout. Most importantly, this approach transforms top-down mentorship into a shared responsibility—and, in doing so, creates a culture where everyone can step up and contribute.

The Future of Mentorship

The evolution becomes clear when we look at it this way:

FROM: Mentorship happens through physical presence.

Built on an apprenticeship model where skills were developed by observing and learning from more-experienced workers, mentorship relied on in-person proximity to leaders. Guidance flowed one way— older to younger—and stayed within the walls of a single company.

TO: Mentorship is accessible to all.

No longer reliant on osmosis, mentorship now blends in-person and digital connection, flows from generation to generation in every direction, and recognizes that no one holds all the answers. The strongest systems link people to peers, leaders, and external networks.

Looking Ahead: A Glimpse of 2050

If we follow this path, what might 2050 look like?

Imagine mentorship as a continuous web that your company helps you build. New technologies and platforms could surface tailored connections in real time: pairing a designer in Chicago with a peer in Singapore who is working to solve a similar problem or matching a young manager with a retired executive-turned-"industry champion" willing to share networks across company lines. Mentorship moments could be captured—as short video snippets, annotated chats, or even immersive simulations—and compiled into a searchable archive, available on demand for those who need to pause, rewind, and learn at their own pace.

But don't miss this: The human element will remain nonnegotiable. Technology can scale access, but only people can bring empathy, candor, and lived experience. By 2050, the best organizations won't just ask, "Who are you learning from at this company?" They'll ask, "How are we connecting you to the people, inside and out, who can help you grow?"

In this version of the future, mentorship is the operating system of work: fluid, multidirectional, and expansive enough to meet the needs of every generation.

So What? Key Takeaways from Chapter 14

This shift—from apprenticeship to accessibility—isn't just about Gen Z. It's about modernizing mentorship for the way every generation works, learns, and connects today. The old model of proximity and hierarchy may have served its time, but in a digital, fast-moving workplace, it's no longer enough.

- **Mentorship isn't disappearing—it's expanding.** The most effective systems blend the depth of in-person connection with the inclusivity and scale of digital access.
- **Guidance is multidirectional.** Wisdom no longer flows only from senior to junior. Peers, younger colleagues, and even external networks now play a critical role.
- **Reverse mentorship isn't about TikTok.** Its power lies in helping older generations master digital body language: clarity, tone, and nuance in a virtual-first world.
- **Gen Z doesn't lack initiative—they just need a starting point.** Leaders can reduce friction by clarifying where to go for help and spreading mentorship across peers, teams, and networks instead of overloading managers.
- **Think beyond your walls.** Sponsorship and championship expand mentorship into the wider industry, creating opportunities that strengthen retention, diversity, and long-term growth.
- **Human connection is still the anchor.** Digital tools can scale knowledge, but empathy, follow-through, and authentic relationships are what make mentorship transformative. But today, leveraging digital tools also help you build that human connection.

15

Shift 10

From Better Answers to Better Questions: Learning in the AI Era

> **The big idea:** In a world where skills expire faster than ever, the real competitive advantage isn't just what you already know—it's pairing that knowledge with the ability to ask better questions and access the right tools, people, and ideas at the right time.

MOST OF THIS book has looked at the systems and leaders shaping change from the top. But systems don't shift unless people do—and learning starts with each of us. This chapter bridges both perspectives: how we learn as individuals and how leaders can design environments that help that learning stick.

As you read, try to keep both lenses in view:

- **Leader lens:** What learning behaviors does my team need—and how can I make them easier to practice?
- **Individual lens:** How do I learn best—and how can I build more of that into my daily work?

Before we dive in, take a quick 60-second pulse check. It's a short quiz to surface your natural learning reflexes. There are no right or wrong answers—just patterns. If you lead others, try it twice: once for yourself, once imagining someone on your team. Your responses will help you see where you are on the spectrum between structure and self-direction—and how that shows up in how you learn, lead, and grow.

Quick Quiz: What Does Great Learning Look Like to You?

Choose the answer that feels most natural:

1. When I need a new skill for work, I expect:
   (a) my company to formally train me.
   (b) to find resources myself and get support when I need it.
2. If I don't know how to do something, my first instinct is to:
   (a) ask someone to explain it to me.
   (b) find a tutorial, how-to YouTube video, report, AI tool, or other resource.
3. I feel most confident learning when:
   (a) there's a clear manual, process, or step-by-step guide.
   (b) I have the autonomy to experiment, ask questions, and discover.
4. For long-term growth, I want my company to:
   (a) provide a clear path for advancement and formal training programs.
   (b) encourage exploration and connect me with tools, people, and ideas on demand.

If you found yourself picking mostly a's: You're in good company. Many professionals prefer structured, company-driven training, especially those who started their careers in an era when formal programs were the norm.

If you leaned toward b's: You're aligned with how learning is evolving for the pace of change today: as self-directed, personalized, digital-first, and rooted in autonomy.

> Neither approach is right or wrong—but, together, they reveal how expectations around learning are evolving and sometimes colliding.

The Learning Myths Holding Us Back

I've observed something important from our research and conversations with industry leaders: Traditionally, learning in the workplace has been about *knowing*: memorizing information, learning facts, and having these ideas at the ready in your head. But for forward-thinking companies today, it's also about *asking*. And that shift is reshaping how we think about training, mentorship, and even how we prepare for the full impact of AI.

That tension—between learning as "having the answers" and learning as "asking better questions"—fuels some of the biggest misconceptions about how people build skills at work. Too many organizations are still stuck following the old playbook: one-off training sessions alone, senior leaders positioned as the ultimate experts, and employees waiting passively to be taught. But that approach alone won't match today's speed of change.

To keep pace in the AI era, we have to bust a few myths about what learning really looks like—and what every generation needs to thrive.

Myth #1: Training Is an Event Limited to a Specific Time and Place

I frequently hear my Gen X peers explain away any knowledge gaps with "I haven't been trained on that," a reflection of our roots in an Encyclopedia Britannica world: Knowledge came in formal doses from authoritative sources. But the Gen Zers in our sessions aren't satisfied with waiting for training. They're frustrated that they can't self-serve answers at work as easily as they can in life outside of work. (For more on this "self-serve" mindset, go back to Chapter 14!)

The data backs this up: 36 percent of organizations still offer training on a monthly cadence, yet only 25 percent of employees actually want it that way.[1] Gen Z is pushing for something different: more frequent, more flexible access. In fact, in a recent survey, 77 percent of Gen Z respondents expressed that they prefer learning via video-based content, which underscores their desire for self-guided skills development.[2] We heard something similar from a Gen Z Cohort participant who told us, "I like to start with videos. I sort of want to give the first round trying myself, and then get it as far as you can, and then you go and ask for help and for it to be reviewed."

Another theme that came up often in our conversations: Gen Zers are eager to practice and apply their new skills. "I learn by doing. If I'm just watching, it doesn't really stick," another session participant explained. "But if I'm hands-on with the project—even if I make mistakes—that's when it clicks."

The lesson: Today's strongest learners today don't wait for the next scheduled class. They try, test, and iterate in real time. Learning is experiential. Companies that make resources searchable, normalize trial and error, and celebrate personal initiative turn learning into a continuous endeavor—and build resilience in the face of constant change. Formal training hasn't disappeared; it's just had a "glow up"—that's a Gen Z term for a positive change for the better.

Myth #2: Knowing the Answers Is What Matters

Yes, we need knowledge to do our job. But, in a fast-changing world, asking better questions matters even more. After all, today's answers expire quickly. What endures are the questions that surface assumptions, constraints, and next steps. When leaders ask great questions, they don't abdicate expertise; they activate critical thinking and autonomy in their teams. It puts people on offense—like runners moving the play forward, rather than receivers waiting for the ball.

Gen Zers we spoke with valued the chance to take a first pass at solving problems themselves—but what they wanted most afterward was context. Other generations have felt this same frustration early in their careers, but it still persists. "I don't need you to just tell me it's wrong and what the right way is," one session participant told us.

"I need to know how and why you got there so I don't make the same mistake moving forward." Another shared the same view: "I don't want someone to just fix the thing for me. I want them to explain why, so the next time I can figure it out myself." If leaders make the effort to ask questions and offer explanations, they can transfer sound judgment and empower employees to go beyond mere task completion.

Leaders who *don't* make the effort will risk missing out on more than just teaching moments. In a *Harvard Business Review* article, one expert urged leaders to reconsider the "overlooked skill" of asking questions. "You think you have the answers to all important questions? That suggests that you are either clueless—you have no idea how rapidly the world is changing—or that you are lying," he warned. "In either case, you won't find that trust that you've been looking for."[3]

The biggest takeaway: Great questions compound learning. They deepen understanding, empower teams to solve problems, and can even prompt leaders to share knowledge they don't even realize they hold. And in the AI era, good prompts are just better questions; they drive stronger reasoning from both humans and machines.

Myth #3: Training Is About Memorization

For too long, training has been treated like cramming for a test: You memorize features, benefits, and protocols and hope they stick. But today, the advantage doesn't come from only holding the answers in your head. It also comes from knowing how to find the right tools, people, and insights at the moment you need them—and, perhaps more importantly, how to connect them across your organization.

Rather than keeping information in silos, AI is enabling more opportunities to capture, catalog, clean, cross-pollinate, and learn from internal knowledge that already exists. A report by MHI and Deloitte highlighted the success of a specialty-materials company that did exactly that.[4] It compiled thousands of digital documents into a curated library and built a Gen AI model that could search, retrieve, and customize answers to employee questions. This move increased productivity by up to 20 percent and operational efficiency by up to 15 percent.

The playbook for organizations is clear: Encourage autonomy, give immediate feedback, and maximize access to internal knowledge by combining catalogued information and opportunities for employees to direct-connect to internal experts. These changes empower employees of all generations to act with speed, confidence, and flexibility.

By debunking these myths, we see that learning today can't be reduced to one-off training events, simplistic answers, or rote memorization. It's bigger than that: The new way forward blends structure and flexibility, digital and human, self-serve and community. The question now is how to design systems that reflect this reality.

The Learning Shift in B2B

This isn't just an internal workplace shift—it has big implications for selling relationships, too.

As a reminder for context: ThinkLab studies these B2B relationships in our industry, focusing on reps selling products to interior designers, such as flooring, furniture, and lighting. Our research found that only 1 percent of Gen Z designers would first consult a trusted rep to learn something new, compared with 16 percent of baby boomers (Figure 15.1). These numbers might *seem* small, but sourcing and

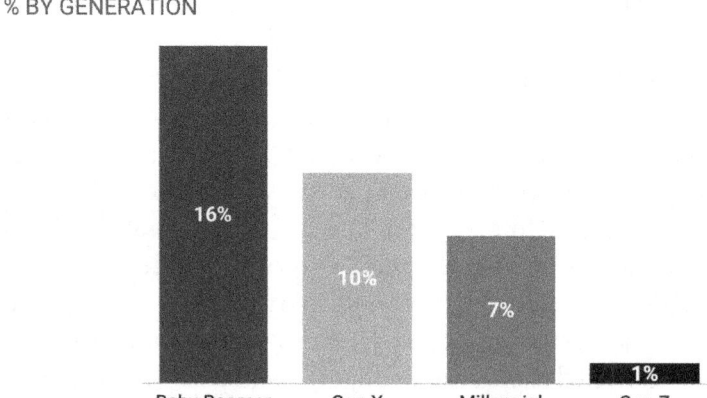

WHO TURNS TO A TRUSTED REP FIRST
% BY GENERATION

Figure 15.1   ThinkLab research shows that for each successive generation, there is a decline in how likely they are to turn to a trusted rep first.

Source: ThinkLab.design Gen Z research / with permission of ThinkLab.

selecting products make up roughly 20 percent of a professional designer's job.

This means that baby boomers rely very heavily on their reps, while Gen Z hardly does at all. And Gen Z designers are often the ones making the primary product selections today. Many reps might shrug this off as a generational quirk. But the real issue isn't *who* the rep is— it's the *why*.

Gen Z (and, increasingly, millennials) don't see the rep as their first stop because many don't understand why that interaction would make their job easier or faster. They won't go to a rep just because tradition dictates that they should. Tomorrow's B2B buyers and influencers demand visible proof of value. To meet that demand, try this:

- **Make expertise tangible.** Don't show up empty-handed. Bring insights they couldn't Google, benchmarks they couldn't access, or shortcuts that save them time.
- **Show; don't tell.** The onus is on reps to demonstrate why connecting with them is the best next step. If engaging with a rep doesn't clearly outperform their own analysis or peer learning, they won't bother.

The message is clear: The future of B2B sales isn't just about being available—it's about being indispensable. And in a digital-first world, that requires integration. If reps continue operating as an isolated analog channel, separate from the digital ecosystems their clients already use, they'll fade into irrelevance. But if they plug in, they can transform into essential partners.

Podcast Insights: "The Age of Lifelong Learning: Insights from Gen Z"

Whether your mind naturally gravitates to a B2B seller or a company trying to upskill its own employees, the best organizations are rethinking learning, moving from one-time training events to continuous, flexible access to skills, people, and ideas. This episode of the *Design Nerds Anonymous* podcast explores this shift in depth:

(continued)

(continued)

- **Learning, education, and training are not interchangeable.** Effective systems braid them together, blending formal instruction with on-demand access.
- **Gen Z highlights the need for a hybrid approach.** Self-serve tools consist of short, digital resources for quick answers. Human connection includes mentorship, shadowing, and peer-based support.
- **Successful programs replace "one-and-done" workshops with experiences.** These ongoing, community-led experiences evolve with changing tools, roles, and industries.

As episode guest and generational researcher Meghan Grace noted: "For a very long time, we looked at learning as this provision of one singular source of knowledge—the trainer, the instructor, the educator—downloading information into the learner." But that's no longer the case: "That power dynamic has shifted. Learners can now guide their own experience and contribute to it," she added.[5]

Learn more about how Gen Z's learning style is affecting the future of corporate training by listening to this DNA podcast.

The Business Case for Rethinking Learning

Today, many professionals fear that AI will take their jobs. But the real risk in the AI era isn't that machines will replace people. It's that organizations will fail to build adaptive learning systems—ones that upskill people rapidly *and motivate them to take part*—will be replaced by those that do.

The pace of change is staggering. A 2025 report by PwC found that the demand for new skills is increasing 66 percent faster in professions heavily impacted by AI, compared with those least impacted.[6] This means that formal credentials and static skill sets go stale almost as soon as they're earned. The same report warns that in AI-exposed roles, knowledge turnover will accelerate, leaving even highly trained employees behind unless companies create pathways for continuous learning.

The World Economic Forum's 2025 report on the future of jobs adds urgency: By 2030, nearly 40 percent of workers' core skills will either change dramatically or become obsolete.[7] For technical and digital roles, the "half-life" of a skill—the time it takes for half of what you know to become irrelevant—is now just two to four years, according to Stanford lecturer Kian Katanforoosh.[8]

The implication is clear: Adaptability is the only sustainable advantage. To thrive, companies need to embed learning into daily work, reward experimentation, and make skill-building as natural as opening a browser tab. But leaders can't carry this load alone. No executive has the intimate knowledge to understand how best to make use of new technology tools in every role. The real breakthroughs come from individual employees—experimenting, asking sharper questions, and testing how these tools can enhance their work.

Upskilling for the Pace of the Future: Practical Ideas for Leaders and Teams

So how do we shift our thinking around learning and upskilling to keep pace with the speed of change? In short, we move from solely relying on structured and company-led training to also include continuous democratized access—a model that fits every generation but is being demanded most loudly by Gen Z.

Let's explore three ways to put that into practice.

Idea #1: Make Asking Questions a Leadership Superpower

We are currently entering an era of "skill instability," and this will raise the importance of soft skills, such as critical thinking, analytical reasoning, resilience, and leadership. In this environment, the true value of leaders comes from knowing how to align the right tools, people, and ideas—and prompting their teams to do the same.

Employers are already making plans in response: 85 percent plan to upskill current workers, 70 percent will hire for new skills, and many intend to redeploy employees internally (reskilling) to stay competitive, according to the World Economic Forum report. In this context, leaders who cling to being the sole source of answers instead of encouraging autonomy risk becoming bottlenecks. Those who embrace asking questions cultivate organizations that adapt in real time and innovate more freely.

Try this:

- **Bake questions into process.** Add a "What did we learn?" prompt to project debriefs.
- **Reward inquiry.** Recognition systems and performance reviews should explicitly value curiosity.
- **Model vulnerability.** When you don't know the answer, say so. Use phrases like "Let's figure this out together" to normalize uncertainty and invite team contributions. If you make a mistake, own it.

This approach has been proven to work: Satya Nadella reshaped Microsoft's culture around what he called being a "learn-it-all" instead of a "know-it-all." Under his leadership, curiosity and questioning became a competitive advantage, fueling both employee engagement and historic business outcomes through record-breaking growth. Since Nadella took over as CEO in 2014, Microsoft has grown from a market cap of $300 billion to more than $3.5 trillion in 2025, making it one of the world's most valuable companies.

Idea #2: Make AI into a Learning Partner, Not Just a Productivity Tool

AI is often framed as a way to get things done faster. But that overlooks another potential benefit: helping people *learn* faster. For decades, corporate training has relied on formal programs or trial and error on the job. AI introduces a third path: a safe, fast practice partner that helps employees practice, iterate, and refine in a low-stakes, self-directed environment.

But AI's potential today isn't limited to efficiency. It's also a source of opportunity: An entry-level designer might search for best practices on pitching creative ideas to a business-oriented audience. A sales rep could rehearse client objections before a pitch. Or a new hire might refine questions to ask to accelerate their onboarding process. None of these scenarios negate the need for humans. Instead, they help employees get to a higher jumping-off point before consulting busy colleagues.

The implication for leaders is clear: If using AI is treated only as a shortcut, employees will miss its role as a skill-building partner. Leaders must deliberately position it as part of a powerful upskilling strategy that works alongside human talent.

Try this:

- **Normalize "AI drills."** Encourage employees to rehearse scenarios with AI: Role-play client conversations, or pressure-test strategies before presenting them live.
- **Pair AI with human feedback.** At times, AI tools can actually discourage workers (especially the youngest ones) from engaging with other humans. To combat this, consider using AI tools as a springboard for coaching opportunities with a human in the loop, reinforcing when and how to lean on human judgment.
- **Reward exploration.** Recognize employees for how they use new tools to upskill themselves.

Here are two examples of companies exploring the use of AI as a learning partner with tangible business results:

- **Walmart** uses AI-powered virtual reality training combined with AI analytics to track employee performance and provide personalized feedback. This approach has improved employee performance by 12.5 percent and reduced training time by 96 percent (from 8 hours to 15 minutes).[9]

■ **Bank of America** leveraged an AI-powered conversation simulation platform to improve the soft skills of their customer service representatives. This effort led to both efficiency gains and higher employee confidence: Participants mastered their training materials more quickly, and 97 percent of trainees in the first year of the program reported that they felt more comfortable performing tasks.[10]

When leaders frame AI as a learning partner, it becomes a catalyst for continuous upskilling—helping employees build confidence, experiment safely, and develop the adaptability that matters most in a world where skills expire quickly.

Idea #3: Make Learning Visible, Connected, and Embedded

Conventional training is something you step away from work to do: a workshop, a certification course, a seminar. But in the future, learning must also be woven directly into the flow of everyday work, enhanced by digital tools but connected to peers, and designed to allow employees to see their own progress.

The leaders who thrive will do three things well. They will make learning embedded, visible, and equitable: Employees can learn in small bursts while doing their jobs, see evidence of their progress, and know they won't be left behind if their starting point is different from that of their peers.

Try this:

■ **Embed learning into workflows.** Deliver microlearning prompts, AI nudges, or "just-in-time" resources inside the tools employees already use. Don't make them go elsewhere.

■ **Make progress visible.** Use digital badges, micro-credentials, or skill dashboards that tie directly to advancement or completion of individual goals.

- **Connect people to people.** Though digital tools are helpful, the real value comes when humans share their learning with other humans. Structure peer cohorts, schedule information exchanges, or create digital channels for practicing skills.
- **Design for equity.** Audit who is—and isn't—taking advantage of learning opportunities. This new digital era risks rewarding those who have had more opportunity to become digitally fluent, so take measures to bring everyone over the threshold: Offer accessible formats, guided on-ramps, or extra support.

The payoff: Employees feel momentum, and organizations see broader participation. As a result, learning stops being an "extracurricular" activity and becomes an everyday part of work.

The Future of Learning

The strategies in this chapter are designed for today, but they also point toward a larger transformation already underway. Here's the shift at the heart of this rule:

FROM: Learning is an event. Knowledge is the goal.

- Information is delivered in scheduled sessions.
- Expertise flows one way: from trainer to trainee.
- Employees wait passively to be taught.
- Leaders are valued for what they know.

TO: Learning is a mindset. Curiosity is the goal.

- Skill-building happens continuously, in real time.
- Exercising discernment matters more than memorization.
- Employees connect with tools, people, and ideas on demand.
- Leaders are valued for asking better questions.

By embracing cultures of curiosity, measured risk-taking, and autonomy, we activate the power of each individual within our organization to move toward a better future.

Looking Ahead: A Glimpse of 2050

If this shift continues, what could corporate learning look like in 2050?

Imagine a world where learning isn't something you *schedule*, but something you *live inside of*. Wearables and AI assistants might gently nudge us throughout the workday with personalized prompts: reminding us to pause, reflect, and build micro-skills into the flow of work.

Every employee might have a dynamic skill map: a living dashboard that tracks abilities they've mastered, highlights skills that are expiring, and suggests new ones to explore. Their devices gamify progress and automatically connect them with small peer cohorts—sometimes colleagues in the same office, sometimes strangers across industries—matched through geolocation or digital spaces for collaboration. Lunch breaks, coffee chats, or quick online huddles become mini-learning labs.

Although experience still matters, leaders will be recognized for how they turn that experience into insight and for the questions they ask: the ones that activate digital tools and unlock insights from the humans around them. Their value lies in sparking curiosity, reframing problems, and prompting more creative answers than any one person could generate alone.

So What? Key Takeaways from Chapter 15

This shift isn't just about training. It's also about redefining how people build skills, how leaders guide, and how organizations keep pace with constant change.

- **Answers matter. Questions multiply their value.** In a world where skills expire quickly, leaders win by asking sharper questions that activate their teams, tools, and surface new insights.
- **Learning is always-on.** The strongest systems embed learning into daily work—blending digital tools, peer connection, and real-time feedback.
- **AI is a practice partner.** When used for drills, simulations, and iteration, AI accelerates confidence and skill-building—not just productivity.
- **First steps matter most.** Lower the threshold for experimentation with buddy systems, gamification, and recognition so people aren't afraid to try.
- **Value is the "why."** Whether inside organizations or in B2B sales, people won't turn to leaders, reps, or tools out of tradition. They'll engage only when it clearly makes their work smarter, better, faster, or easier.

Conclusion

WORK MAY FEEL broken, but it isn't beyond repair. The cracks we see—those struggles to connect our teams across generations, digital divides, and expanding geographies—are signs that our systems are still running on defaults built for another era.

Throughout this book, we've taken a look at the impact of following those defaults: burnout, trust eroded by miscommunication, cultures tethered to place instead of people, mentorship models that depend on osmosis, and even learning systems still designed for memorization over adaptability. Each shift revealed the same truth: The way we worked yesterday can't carry us into tomorrow without intentional rework.

We can only make a real breakthrough when we stop trying to patch those old systems and instead ask: *What do we want work to be now?* That's where Gen Z workers offer us an edge—not because they have all the answers, but because they don't carry the same baggage.

While many other generations faced similar challenges early in their careers, the context has changed. The world is now changing faster than ever before. Gen Zers naturally see the world from a lens that none of us elders had. They are digital-first by default, they came of age in a pandemic, and they expect work to blend with life in ways that our previous models could never accommodate. Their perspective helps us see long-standing problems with fresh eyes, while the lived experience of older generations helps us recognize patterns, avoid hard-earned mistakes, and carry forward what still works. As more of that experience begins to exit the workforce as Boomers retire, how we connect across generations matters more than ever.

Let's review what we've learned as we reexamined our old systems:

- **There's a growing trust gap.** Professionals are experiencing an erosion of trust with their colleagues. This growing trust gap is driven by miscommunication across generations, geographies, and levels of digital fluency. It's more than a business problem—it's a cultural one.
- **Now is the time to rethink the rules around work.** The unspoken norms shaping how we work were built for a world that no longer exists. If we don't pause to question the rules we've inherited, we'll keep reinforcing the very problems we're trying to solve.
- **It starts with individuals.** Before we can redesign knowledge work for the better, we must redefine what *better* means. Most of us spent years in 9-to-5 office jobs without asking when, where, or what makes us most productive. Take the time to identify those preferences and trade-offs. Clarity with ourselves is the first step to reshaping better work lives.
- **Companies can't fix a *how* problem with a *where* solution.** To keep up with the speed of change, companies must stop designing policies for the workforce they *used* to have—and start building systems for the talent they want to *keep and attract next*.
- **Fresh ideas require new inputs.** In a world moving faster than ever, your biggest competitive advantage is fresh perspective. Innovation doesn't come from echo chambers. It comes from building systems that surface unseen ideas—and leaders bold enough to hear them.

Together we explored how cross-generational research and ideas from Gen Z suggest we can solve the following business challenges. Here are the summarized big ideas from all 10 shifts:

- **TRUST and CONNECTION:**
  - o **Shift 1 | Shift from a physical to "phygital" mindset.** In an increasingly digital world, the real competitive advantage isn't choosing between remote and in-person work—it's learning to use one to reinforce the other. Digital sparks connection; face-to-face makes it stick.
  - o **Shift 2 | Build trust through authenticity online and off.** In a world where everyone can see behind the curtain, trust comes from clarity, consistency, and authenticity—not perfection. Show up the same way online and in person, and you'll earn the only real competitive advantage: the trust of your employees and customers.
- **RECRUIT and RETAIN:**
  - o **Shift 3 | Reframe your recruiting process to build trust from the start.** In a world where employees expect purpose and personalization from day one, the companies that win aren't running longer hiring processes—they're running smarter ones. The best recruiting today builds trust, clarity, and connection from very first click.
  - o **Shift 4 | Recognize that the rules to retain now revolve around mutual benefit.** Loyalty isn't dead—it's just more discerning now. In a world where employees have more access to opportunities, options, and information than ever before, the real question isn't *"Why are they leaving?"* It's *"Why would they stay?"* People stay where they grow—and leave when their growth stalls.
- **CULTURE and PURPOSE:**
  - o **Shift 5 | Grow culture by combining microcultures.** We've shifted from culture-as-a-place to culture-as-a-network: a web of microcultures built on trust, shared norms, and belonging. Like strands of a rope, these groups are stronger together, powering performance and keeping people connected no matter where they work.

o **Shift 6 | Define customizable career paths that fuel purpose and create impact.** We are at risk of a leadership pipeline crisis because younger generations demand that we define career success differently. Titles, status, or corner offices are no longer the sole motivators. Instead, Gen Zers set a premium on purpose and autonomy—and prioritizing their well-being along the way.

- **COLLABORATION and COMMUNICATION:**
  o **Shift 7 | Fuel collaboration through a balanced blend of synch and asynch.** In a world drowning in meetings, more time together doesn't necessarily equal more progress. The best teams today balance synchronous and asynchronous collaboration, using live time for alignment and decision-making, and async tools to make space for deep thinking and follow-through.
  o **Shift 8 | Expand impact and alignment through better communication.** In a world of bigger teams, shorter attention spans, and fewer chances to be in the room, the leaders who win aren't saying more—they're saying it clearer. The best communication today is bite-sized, shareable, and designed to travel without you.
- **MENTORSHIP and LEARNING:**
  o **Shift 9 | Make mentorship multidirectional, multidimensional, and accessible to all.** Today's strongest cultures don't rely on osmosis for mentorship—they make guidance accessible. By blending digital tools with human connection, leaders can reimagine mentorship to flow across generations, extend beyond company walls, and strengthen careers at every stage.
  o **Shift 10 | Blend training events with empowered learning cultures.** In a world where skills expire faster than ever, the real competitive advantage isn't just what you already know—it's pairing that knowledge with the ability to ask better questions and access the right tools, people, and ideas at the right time.

So, where do we go from here? This is not a story of one generation rescuing another. It's about all of us doing our part to design work cultures that actually work for the era we live in today.

Here are the most important actions each of us can take, as laid out in this book:

- **Individual workers:** No one can design a better approach to work until we each define what "better" means for ourselves. So, start by getting clear on where, when, and how you work best, then put it into practice: Complete the exercises in Chapter 3, and experiment with the communication shifts outlined in this book.
- **Managers:** Managers sit on the front lines of change. Your job is to model these shifts with radical openness and to test and iterate in real time. In doing so, you activate your team to believe a better way of working is possible—and prove it to senior leadership.
- **HR leaders:** Turn successful experiments into policies that can benefit all teams. Support frontline managers, take what works from their tests, and build it into policies that are rewarded, reinforced, and scaled across the organization.
- **CEOs and senior leaders:** The future of work will rise or fall on your willingness to lead differently. Retire the old playbook, amplify what's working, and include fresh voices in decision-making so that the workplace we pass down to the next generation is one worth inheriting.
- **B2B partners:** The selling process is being rewritten. Your greatest value now is to harness digital tools for scale while identifying the latent needs in the organizations you serve and meeting them with the insight and perspective that make you, as a human, indispensable.

Together, these shifts reveal a simple truth: The future of work won't be mandated by leaders at the top or dictated by a single generation. It will be co-created—through experiments, prototypes, and the courage to replace outdated norms with systems that reflect who we are today and who we want to become tomorrow.

At the time of writing, our world of work feels stuck in a kind of purgatory. We can't go back to the old ways. But we also can't yet fully see what's next on the horizon.

That uncertainty is real. We feel it in our overscheduled calendars, in our now-more-notable-than-before commutes, in the fatigue of trying to keep up with technologies that change faster than we do. And yet, I've also come to believe that what feels like purgatory is actually a passage. It's the messy middle we have to move through to get somewhere new and better.

Gen Zers are now demanding to follow the same principles that sustained me when my own work life wasn't working. These demands aren't a request for special treatment, but instead point us *all* toward a healthier (and, ironically, more human) way forward. Their impatience, their questions, their insistence on work–life balance and purpose: These qualities exemplify Gen Zers. But these aren't generational quirks. They are guideposts.

If we truly listen and use these fresh inputs to prototype new ways of working, we unlock something invaluable: workplaces that actually work—for companies, for leaders and teams, for seasoned talent and new hires, for parents, caretakers, and future generations we haven't even met yet.

Work is broken. Gen Z can fix it, but it will take all of us to make it happen.

And that's where this book ends—but also where the work begins.

Notes

Chapter 1

1. "Remote Work, Hybrid Work, In-Office Work Forecast," Global Marketplace Analytics, accessed September 30, 2025, https://globalwork placeanalytics.com/work-at-home-after-covid-19-our-forecast.
2. "Winter 2022/2023 Future Forum Pulse: Amid Spiking Burnout, Workplace Flexibility Fuels Company Culture and Productivity," Future Forum, February 15, 2023, https://futureforum.com/wp-content/uploads/2023/02/Future-Forum-Pulse-Report-Winter-2022-2023.pdf.
3. "State of Hybrid Work 2025: United States," Owl Labs, September 23, 2025, https://owllabs.com/state-of-hybrid-work/2025.
4. "State of the Global Workplace: Understanding Employees, Informing Leaders," Gallup, April 22, 2025, https://www.gallup.com/workplace/349484/state-of-the-global-workplace.aspx.
5. "Indicators: Hybrid Work," Gallup, last accessed September 30, 2025, https://www.gallup.com/401384/indicator-hybrid-work.aspx#ite-510890.
6. Amanda Schneider, Erica Waayenberg, and Allison Roon, "Unlocking Gen Z's Potential to Impact the Future of Work," ThinkLab, last accessed September 30, 2025, https://info.thinklab.design/gen-z-research.
7. "ThinkLab's 2025 Gen Z Cohort Initiative," ThinkLab, last accessed September 30, 2025, https://info.thinklab.design/genzcohort.

Chapter 2

1. "Work Trend Index Annual Report: Will AI Fix Work?" Microsoft, May 9, 2023, https://www.microsoft.com/en-us/worklab/work-trend-index/will-ai-fix-work.

2. "State of the Global Workplace: Understanding Employees, Informing Leaders," Gallup, April 22, 2025, https://www.gallup.com/workplace/349484/state-of-the-global-workplace.aspx.

3. Sarah DeGue, Robyn Singleton, and Megan Kearns, "A Qualitative Analysis of Beliefs About Masculinity and Gender Socialization Among U.S. Mothers and Fathers of School-Age Boys," *Psychology of Men & Masculinities* 25, no. 2 (October 5, 2023): 152–164, https://doi.org/10.1037/men0000450.

4. *"Suicide Data and Statistics,"* Centers for Disease Control and Prevention, March 26, 2025, https://www.cdc.gov/suicide/facts/data.html.

5. Natalia Vega Varela and Leyly Moridi, "The Free-Time Gender Gap: How Unpaid Care and Household Labor Reinforces Women's Inequality," Gender Equity Policy Institute, October 2024, https://www.doi.org/10.5281/zenodo.14207518.

6. Amanda Schneider, *"Work Is Broken. Gen Z Can Help Fix It,"* TED Talk, Fargo, ND, July 2024, 12 min., 11 sec., https://www.ted.com/talks/amanda_schneider_work_is_broken_gen_z_can_help_fix_it_mar_2025.

Chapter 3

1. Ian Page, Kevin Reuss, and Zoë Zemper, *"Changes in the U.S. Labor Supply,"* Trendlines, U.S. Department of Labor Employment and Training Administration, August 2024, https://www.dol.gov/sites/dolgov/files/ETA/opder/DASP/Trendlines/posts/2024_08/Trendlines_August_2024.html.

2. Ang Richard, "Generation Z in the Workplace," National Association of Colleges and Employers, January 16, 2024, https://www.naceweb.org/talent-acquisition/student-attitudes/generation-z-in-the-workplace.

3. Hannah Grady Williams, *A Leader's Guide to Unlocking Gen Z: Insider Strategies to Empower Your Team* (Black Balsam Press, 2021).

4. Elizabeth Faber, "Gen Zs and Millennials at Work: Pursuing a Balance of Money, Meaning, and Well-Being," Deloitte, June 2, 2025, https://www.deloitte.com/us/en/insights/topics/talent/2025-gen-z-millennial-survey.html.

Chapter 4

1. Amanda Schneider, host, *Design Nerds Anonymous* podcast, season 6, episode 7, "The Future of Work: An Entanglement of IT, HR, and Design," ThinkLab, November 12, 2024, https://insights.thinklab. design/the-future-of-work-an-entanglement-of-it-hr-and-desig.

2. Anne Marie D. Lee, "America Is Hitting 'Peak 65' in 2024 as Record Number of Boomers Reach Retirement Age. Here's What to Know," *CBS News*, January 29, 2024, https://www.cbsnews.com/news/retirement-medicare-401k-what-to-know-peak-65/.

3. "By 2030, All Baby Boomers Will Be Age 65 or Older," United States Census Bureau, December 10, 2019, https://www.census.gov/library/stories/ 2019/12/by-2030-all-baby-boomers-will-be-age-65-or-older.html.

4. "The Generations Defined," McCrindle, accessed July 31, 2025, https:// mccrindle.com.au/article/topic/demographics/the-generations-defined.

5. Annabel Burba, "Gen-Z Trusts Social Media for Financial Advice More Than Any Other Generation," *Inc.*, May 19, 2025, https://www.inc.com/ annabel-burba/gen-z-trusts-social-media-for-financial-advice-more-than-any-other-generation/91189521.

6. Denise McLain and Ryan Pendell, "Why Trust in Leaders Is Faltering and How to Gain It Back," Gallup, April 17, 2023, https://www.gallup .com/workplace/473738/why-trust-leaders-faltering-gain-back.aspx.

7. Amanda Schneider, host, *Design Nerds Anonymous* podcast, season 5, episode 1, "Redefining Office Culture," ThinkLab, September 7, 2023, https://insights.thinklab.design/dna-podcast-redefining-office-culture.

8. "Unveiling *Interior Design*'s 2025 Top 100 Giants," *Interior Design*, March 17, 2025, https://interiordesign.net/research/interior-designs-2025-top-100-giants/.

9. Amanda Schneider, host, *Design Nerds Anonymous* podcast, season 6, episode 5, "Why Traditional Workplace Metrics Are Obsolete," ThinkLab, October 24, 2024, https://insights.thinklab.design/why-traditional-workplace-metrics-are-obsolete.

10. Amanda Schneider, host, *Design Nerds Anonymous* podcast, season 7, episode 2, "The Future of Work: Corporate Collaboration in the Phygital Landscape," ThinkLab, April 10, 2025, https://insights.thinklab.design/ the-future-of-work-corporate-collaboration-in-the-phygital-landscape.

Chapter 5

1. Jennifer Jordan and Michael Sorell, "Why You Should Create a 'Shadow Board' of Younger Employees," *Harvard Business Review*, June 4, 2019, https://hbr.org/2019/06/why-you-should-create-a-shadow-board-of-younger-employees.

2. Erica Waayenberg, "2025 U.S. Design Industry Benchmark Report: Trends in Regional Growth, Technology, and Client Expectations," ThinkLab, January 24, 2025, https://insights.thinklab.design/2025-u.s.-design-industry-benchmark-report-trends-in-regional-growth-technology-and-client-expectations.

3. Benita N. Chatmon et al., "Younger Nurses Seek Belonging, Leadership Opportunities, Solutions for Workplace Challenges," *American Nurse Journal*, October 3, 2024, https://www.myamericannurse.com/creating-an-organization-for-future-generations.

4. Jennifer Jordan and Michael Sorell, "Why You Should Create a 'Shadow Board' of Younger Employees," *Harvard Business Review*, June 4, 2019, https://hbr.org/2019/06/why-you-should-create-a-shadow-board-of-younger-employees.

5. Hugh Macquarrie et al., "Leading a Multigenerational Workforce with a Junior Advisory Board," Deloitte, September 28, 2023, https://www.deloitte.com/ch/en/services/consulting/perspectives/leading-a-multigenerational-workforce-with-a-junior-advisory-board.html.

6. Scott Millar, "Four of the Most Innovative Youth Advisory Boards Around the World," last modified January 9, 2024, https://www.iamscottmillar.com/post/four-of-the-most-innovative-youth-advisory-boards-around-the-world.

7. Juliana Kaplan and Rebecca Knight, "Gen Z Wants to Run Your Company. 'Shadow Boards' Give Them a Say Without Handing Them the Keys," *Business Insider*, March 31, 2023, https://www.businessinsider.com/oliver-wyman-shadow-board-young-workers-genz-retention-2023-3.

8. "National Population by Characteristics: 2020–2024," U.S. Census Bureau, June 2025, https://www.census.gov/data/tables/time-series/demo/popest/2020s-national-detail.html.

Chapter 6

1. Hannah Grady Williams, *A Leader's Guide to Unlocking Gen Z: Insider Strategies to Empower Your Team* (Black Balsam Press, 2021).
2. Amanda Schneider, host, *Design Nerds Anonymous* podcast, season 5, episode 8, "Fostering Authentic Relationships with Gen Z," ThinkLab, October 26, 2023, https://insights.thinklab.design/dna-podcast-fostering-authentic-relationships-with-gen-z.
3. Ryan Pendell and Sangeeta Agrawal, "Fully Remote Work Least Popular with Gen Z," Gallup, July 23, 2025, https://www.gallup.com/workplace/692675/fully-remote-work-least-popular-gen-z.aspx.
4. "Unlocking Gen Z's Potential to Impact the Future of Work," ThinkLab, last accessed September 30, 2025, https://info.thinklab.design/gen-z-research.

Chapter 7

1. "Annual Benefit Corporation Report: Fiscal Year 2021," Patagonia, February 25, 2022, https://www.patagonia.com/on/demandware.static/-/Library-Sites-PatagoniaShared/default/dwc42c0028/PDF-US/PAT_2021_BCorp_Report-REV.pdf.
2. "2025 Edelman Trust Barometer: Trust and the Crisis of Grievance," Edelman Trust Institute, January 17, 2025, https://www.edelman.com/sites/g/files/aatuss191/files/2025-01/2025%20Edelman%20Trust%20Barometer_Final.pdf.
3. "ACLC National Poll Shows Generational Differences in Leadership Needs," Allegacy Center for Leadership and Character at the Wake Forest School of Business, accessed on September 30, 2025, https://clc.business.wfu.edu/article/aclc-national-poll-shows-generational-differences-in-leadership-needs.
4. Sarah Goff-Dupont, "In Their Own Words: Growing Up Open," Atlassian, April 18, 2019, https://www.atlassian.com/blog/teamwork/staying-open-at-scale.
5. Michael Bright, "Imagine if B2C companies hid information like the average B2B SaaS website," LinkedIn, January 12, 2022, https://www.linkedin.com/posts/michael-bright-63314332_imagine-if-b2c-companies-hid-information-activity-6887085055718629376-IUBP.
6. Amanda Schneider, host, *Design Nerds Anonymous*, season 4, episode 4, "How to Build Trust with B2B Clients in Today's Digitally Transparent

Era," ThinkLab, October 20, 2022, https://insights.thinklab.design/what-most-companies-get-wrong-online-presence-strategies-in-the-digital-first-era.

7. Liz Harrison et al., "*B2B Sales: Omnichannel Everywhere, Every Time,*" McKinsey & Company, December 15, 2021, https://www.mckinsey.com/capabilities/growth-marketing-and-sales/our-insights/b2b-sales-omnichannel-everywhere-every-time.

Chapter 8

1. Ana Kreacic, John Romeo, and Lucia Uribe, "How to Recruit Generation Z Workers—And Keep Them," World Economic Forum, January 16, 2023, https://www.weforum.org/stories/2023/01/how-to-recruit-generation-z-workers-and-keep-them-davos23/.

2. S. J. Niderost, "10 Takeaways From the 2025 Recruiting Benchmarks Report," Gem, January 16, 2025, https://www.gem.com/blog/10-takeaways-from-the-2025-recruiting-benchmarks-report.

3. "Greenhouse State of Job Hunting 2024," Greenhouse, https://grnhse-marketing-site-assets.s3.amazonaws.com/production/Greenhouse_State_Of_Job_Hunting_Report_Infographic_2024.pdf.

4. "Recruiting Benchmarks 2025," SmartRecruiters and Lighthouse Research & Advisory, July 29, 2025, https://ta.smartrecruiters.com/rs/664-NIC-529/images/Recruitment-Benchmarks-2025-Report.pdf.

5. Jeff Gillis and Mike Simpson, "Swipe Up to Hire Me: Why Gen Z Is Replacing PDFs with 60-Second TikTok Resumes (and How to Film Yours)," *The Interview Guys* (blog), May 9, 2025, https://blog.theinterviewguys.com/tiktok-resumes.

6. "Deloitte's 2023 Gen Z and Millennial Survey Reveals Workplace Progress Despite New Setbacks," Deloitte, May 17, 2023, https://www.deloitte.com/global/en/about/press-room/2023-gen-z-and-millenial-survey.html.

Chapter 9

1. "Millennials or Gen Z: Who's Doing the Most Job-Hopping," Career-Builder, October 5, 2021, https://www.careerbuilder.com/advice/blog/how-long-should-you-stay-in-a-job.

2. Anu Madgavk et al., "Human Capital at Work: The Value of Experience," McKinsey Global Institute, June 2, 2022, https://www.mckinsey.com/

capabilities/people-and-organizational-performance/our-insights/
human-capital-at-work-the-value-of-experience.

3. "The Future of Jobs Report 2025," World Economic Forum, January 7, 2025, https://reports.weforum.org/docs/WEF_Future_of_Jobs_Report_2025.pdf.

4. Natasha Piñon, "How Payscale Improved Talent Retention with Pay Transparency," CFO Brew, June 27, 2023, https://www.cfobrew.com/stories/2023/06/27/the-startup-that-shared-everything.

5. Amy Spurling, "Case Study: The Value of Pay Transparency and How to Implement It," People Managing People, last modified December 6, 2024, https://peoplemanagingpeople.com/payroll-compensation/pay-transparency-compt.

6. Leon Lam et al., "Research: The Unintended Consequences of Pay Transparency," *Harvard Business Review*, August 12, 2022, https://hbr.org/2022/08/research-the-unintended-consequences-of-pay-transparency.

Chapter 10

1. Radostina Purvanova and Alanah Mitchell, "US Workers with Remote-Friendly Jobs Are Still Working from Home Nearly Half the Time, 5 Years After the Pandemic Began," *The Conversation*, March 12, 2025, https://theconversation.com/us-workers-with-remote-friendly-jobs-are-still-working-from-home-nearly-half-the-time-5-years-after-the-pandemic-began-251758.

2. Sabrina Wulff Pabilonia and Jill Janocha Redmond, "The Rise in Remote Work Since the Pandemic and Its Impact on Productivity," *Beyond the Numbers 13*, no. 8 (October 2024), Bureau of Labor Statistics, https://www.bls.gov/opub/btn/volume-13/remote-work-productivity.htm.

3. Lillio Mok et al., "Challenging but Connective: Large-Scale Characteristics of Synchronous Collaboration Across Time Zones," paper presented at 2023 CHI Conference on Human Factors in Computing Systems, Hamburg, Germany, April 23–28, 2023, https://dl.acm.org/doi/10.1145/3544548.3581141.

4. Brian Westfall, "Overcoming Time Differences, Language Barriers, and Culture Clashes to Optimize Global Team Collaboration," Capterra, March 20, 2024, https://www.capterra.com/resources/global-team-collaboration.

5. John Pitonyak and Rob DeSimone, "How to Engage Frontline Managers," Gallup, updated January 19, 2024, https://www.gallup.com/workplace/395210/engage-frontline-managers.aspx.

6. Amanda Schneider, host, *Design Nerds Anonymous* podcast, season 6, episode 8, "Generation Gap: Rethinking Soft Skills in the Hybrid Workplace," ThinkLab, November 21, 2024, https://insights.thinklab.design/generation-gap-rethinking-soft-skills-in-the-hybrid-workplace.

7. Brian Elliott et al., *How the Future Works: Leading Flexible Teams to Do the Best Work of Their Lives* (Wiley, 2022).

8. "Team-Level Agreements: Customizable Template," Future Forum, October 2021, https://futureforum.com/wp-content/uploads/2021/10/Future-Forum-Team-level-Agreements-Template.pdf.

9. Alison Beard, host, *HBR IdeaCast* podcast, episode 948, "Supercharge Your One-on-One Meetings," *Harvard Business Review*, January 9, 2024, https://hbr.org/podcast/2024/01/supercharge-your-one-on-one-meetings.

10. Patrick Lencioni's *The 6 Types of Working Genius: A Better Way to Understand Your Gifts, Your Frustrations, and Your Team* (Matt Holt Books, 2022).

Chapter 11

1. "2025 Gen Z and Millennial Survey: Growth and the Pursuit of Money, Meaning, and Well-Being," Deloitte, May 8, 2025, https://www.deloitte.com/content/dam/assets-shared/docs/campaigns/2025/2025-genz-millennial-survey.pdf.

2. "Why Gen Z Is Redefining the Workplace with 'Career Minimalism'," Glassdoor, August 26, 2025, https://www.glassdoor.com/blog/why-gen-z-is-redefining-work.

3. "The Next-Gen Workforce: Five Key Tech Areas Separate Younger Workers from Older Generations," Forrester, March 16, 2021, https://www.forrester.com/press-newsroom/the-next-gen-workforce-five-key-tech-areas-separate-younger-workers-from-older-generations.

4. "The Authenticity Imperative: How Gen Z's Values Are Reshaping Leadership Paradigms," Horton International, https://hortoninternational.com/how-genz-values-are-reshaping-leadership-paradigms.

5. Valeria Cox, "Why Millennials and Gen Z Don't Want to Lead: The C-Suite Crisis Ahead," Stanton Chase, August 2025, https://www.stantonchase.com/insights/blog/why-millennials-and-gen-z-dont-want-to-lead-the-c-suite-crisis-ahead.

6. Bryan Robinson, "Job Burnout at 66% in 2025, New Study Shows," *Forbes*, February 8, 2025, https://www.forbes.com/sites/bryanrobinson/2025/02/08/job-burnout-at-66-in-2025-new-study-shows.

7. Amanda Schneider, host, *Design Nerds Anonymous* podcast, Gen Z series, episode 4, "How to Keep Gen Z from Leaving the Design Industry," ThinkLab, March 30, 2023, https://insights.thinklab.design/dna-podcast-how-to-keep-gen-z-from-leaving-the-design-industry.

8. Amanda Schneider, host, *Design Nerds Anonymous* podcast, season 5, episode 6, "Gamify Career Paths for Gen Z," ThinkLab, October 12, 2023, https://insights.thinklab.design/dna-podcast-gamify-career-paths-for-gen-z.

9. Amanda Schneider, host, *Design Nerds Anonymous* podcast, season 5, episode 7, "Igniting Purpose at Work: Inspiring Employees," ThinkLab, October 19, 2023, https://insights.thinklab.design/dna-podcast-igniting-purpose-at-work-inspiring-employees.

10. Angela Henshall, "Can the 'Right to Disconnect' Exist in a Remote-Work World?" BBC, May 21, 2021, https://www.bbc.com/worklife/article/20210517-can-the-right-to-disconnect-exist-in-a-remote-work-world.

11. "Volkswagen AG Revenue 2010–2025 | VWAGY," Macrotrends, accessed on September 10, 2025, https://www.macrotrends.net/stocks/charts/VWAGY/volkswagen-ag/revenue.

12. Morgan Smith, "This U.S. Company Tested a 4-Day Workweek—and Says It Made Workers Happier and More Productive," CNBC, April 5, 2024, https://www.cnbc.com/2024/04/05/exos-4-day-workweek-how-it-went-one-year-later.html.

13. David Brooks, *The Second Mountain: The Quest for a Moral Life* (Random House, 2019).

Chapter 12

1. "Meetings Statistics: How Many Hours Do We Spend in Meetings?" Fellow, https://fellow.ai/blog/meetings-statistics-how-many-hours-do-we-spend-in-meetings.

2. "Work Trend Index Annual Report: Will AI Fix Work?" Microsoft, May 9, 2023, https://www.microsoft.com/en-us/worklab/work-trend-index/will-ai-fix-work.

3. "Smart Meetings Trends Report," Reclaim.ai, April 23, 2024, https://reclaim.ai/blog/smart-meetings-report.

4. Julia Szatar, "When to Choose Synchronous vs. Asynchronous Communication," Atlassian, November 17, 2022, https://www.atlassian .com/blog/loom/synchronous-vs-asynchronous.

5. Amanda Schneider, host, *Design Nerds Anonymous* podcast, season 5, episode 2, "Sparking Creativity in a Digital World," ThinkLab, September 14, 2023, https://insights.thinklab.design/design-nerds-anonymous-sparking-creativity-in-a-digital-world.

6. "Research Proves Your Brain Needs Breaks," Microsoft, April 20, 2021, https://www.microsoft.com/en-us/worklab/work-trend-index/brain-research.

7. Petri Lehtonen, "The Cost of Poor-Quality Meetings: A Deep Dive into the Data," Flowtrace, May 21, 2023, https://www.flowtrace.co/collaboration-blog/the-cost-of-poor-quality-meetings-a-deep-dive-into-the-data.

8. "Workplace Woes: Meetings Edition," Atlassian, March 2024, https://www.atlassian.com/blog/workplace-woes-meetings.

9. Murphy Jr, Bill "Google Says It Still Uses the '20 Percent Rule,' and You Should Totally Copy It," *Inc.*, November 1, 2020, https://www.inc.com/bill-murphy-jr/google-says-it-still-uses-20-percent-rule-you-should-totally-copy-it.html.

10. David Gurteen, "The Google 20% Free Time Policy," *Conversational Leadership*, accessed on September 15, 2025, conversational-leadership .net/google-free-time-policy.

11. Jens Schumacher, "Innovation Week: 20% Time in a Box," Atlassian, September 10, 2012, https://www.atlassian.com/blog/archives/innovation-week-20-time-in-a-box$.

12. Sheryl Estrada, "Shopify's CFO Explains How Its New Meeting Cost Calculator Works, and How It Will Cut 474,000 Events in 2023: 'Time Is Money,'" *Fortune*, July 14, 2023, https://fortune.com/2023/07/14/shopify-cfo-meeting-cost-calculator.

13. "2025: The Year the Frontier Firm Was Born," Microsoft, April 23, 2025, https://www.microsoft.com/en-us/worklab/work-trend-index/2025-the-year-the-frontier-firm-is-born.

Chapter 13

1. Mike Hege (@mikehege.realtor), "Help, she said I was cringe 😭 @PridemoreProperties #fyp #breathingguy #breathingrealtor #inhale #genzedit #genzhumor," TikTok post, July 11, 2024, https://www.tiktok .com/@mikehege.realtor/video/7390480203392372010.

2. "Capturing Attention in Feed: The Science Behind Effective Video Creative," Facebook IQ, April 20, 2016, https://www.facebook.com/business/news/insights/capturing-attention-feed-video-creative.

3. Gloria Mark, *Attention Span: A Groundbreaking Way to Restore Balance, Happiness and Productivity* (Hanover Square Press, 2023).

4. Barbara Winters et al., "The State of Business Buying, 2024," Forrester, December 3, 2024, https://www.forrester.com/report/the-state-of-business-buying-2024/RES181797.

5. "5 Paradigm Shifts Reshaping End-User Decision Making," ThinkLab, June 25, 2025, https://info.thinklab.design/enduserdecisionmaking.

6. Amanda Schneider, host, *Design Nerds Anonymous* podcast, season 6, episode 3, "Managing Up: Today's Crucial Skill You Weren't Taught," ThinkLab, October 10, 2024, https://insights.thinklab.design/managing-up-todays-crucial-skill-you-werent-taught.

7. Judy T. Lin et al., *"Financial Capability in the United States: Results from the FINRA Foundation's National Financial Capability Study,"* 6th edition, FINRA Investor Education Foundation, July 2025, www.FINRA Foundation.org/NFCSReport2024.

Chapter 14

1. Amanda Schneider, host, *Design Nerds Anonymous* podcast, season 5, episode 1, "Redefining Office Culture," ThinkLab, September 7, 2023, https://insights.thinklab.design/dna-podcast-redefining-office-culture.

2. Nicole Kobie, "'Reverse Mentorship': How Young Workers Are Teaching Bosses," BBC, November 14, 2022, https://www.bbc.com/worklife/article/20221110-reverse-mentorship-how-young-workers-are-teaching-bosses.

3. Kevin S. Dubina, "Labor Force and Macroeconomic Projections Overview and Highlights, 2023–33," *Monthly Labor Review*, U.S. Bureau of Labor Statistics, August 29, 2024, https://www.bls.gov/opub/mlr/2024/article/labor-force-and-macroeconomic-projections-overview-and-highlights-2023-33.htm.

4. Amanda Schneider, host, *Design Nerds Anonymous* podcast, season 5, episode 3, "Is Mentorship Dead?" ThinkLab, September 21, 2023, https://insights.thinklab.design/design-nerds-anonymous-is-mentorship-dead.

Chapter 15

1. "2022 Workplace Learning & Development Trends," SHRM, August 17, 2022, https://www.shrm.org/content/dam/en/shrm/research/2022-Workplace-Learning-and Development-Trends-Report.pdf.
2. Allyson Fowler, "New Data: Millennials and Gen Z Employees Demand Skill Development," Seismic, April 2, 2025, https://www.seismic.com/blog/millennials-gen-z-demand-skill-development.
3. John III Hagel, "Good Leadership Is About Asking Good Questions," *Harvard Business Review*, January 8, 2021, https://hbr.org/2021/01/good-leadership-is-about-asking-good-questions.
4. Carol Miller et al., "The Collaborative Chain: 2024 MHI Annual Industry Report," MHI and Deloitte, March 12, 2024, https://og.mhi.org/publications/report.
5. Amanda Schneider, host, *Design Nerds Anonymous* podcast, season 5, episode 5, "The Age of Lifelong Learning: Insights from Gen Z," ThinkLab, October 5, 2023, https://insights.thinklab.design/dna-podcast-the-age-of-lifelong-learning-insights-from-gen-z.
6. "The Fearless Future: 2025 Global AI Jobs Barometer," PwC, June 3, 2025, https://www.pwc.com/gx/en/issues/artificial-intelligence/job-barometer/2025/report.pdf.
7. "Future of Jobs Report 2025," World Economic Forum, January 2025, https://reports.weforum.org/docs/WEF_Future_of_Jobs_Report_2025.pdf.
8. Joe McKendrick, "AI Puts the Squeeze on the Shrinking Half-life of Skills," *Forbes*, April 30, 2024, https://www.forbes.com/sites/joemckendrick/2024/04/30/ai-puts-the-squeeze-on-the-shrinking-half-life-of-skills.
9. Rebekah Carter, "Immersive Learning Case Studies: XR Training Success Stories," *XR Today*, March 13, 2025, https://www.xrtoday.com/virtual-reality/immersive-learning-case-studies-xr-training-success-stories.
10. Katherine Doherty, "Bank of America Is Using AI and Metaverse to Train New Hires," *Bloomberg News*, July 13, 2023, https://www.bloomberg.com/news/articles/2023-07-13/bank-of-america-is-using-the-metaverse-ai-to-train-its-hires.

Acknowledgments

THIS BOOK WAS not created alone. It grew from years of conversation, curiosity, collaboration—and from the circle of people who surrounded me through it all.

When I think about that circle, I'm reminded of a story that's always stayed with me—one about the way female elephants rally around their tribe of women: when one is stressed or injured, the others form a protective circle around her, kicking up dust to mask her fear pheromones from predators. Likewise, when she gives birth, the circle again surrounds her trumpeting in celebration. That image captures exactly how I've felt supported, both personally and professionally, by my own circle of women not just throughout the writing of this book, but life. Sometimes I've been the one in the middle; sometimes I've been the one fiercely kicking up dust. But my circle of sisterhood has always remained.

First, to my parents, who taught me that girls could do anything boys could do—and to my elephant circle of women, who have spent decades proving it true. You challenged me, celebrated me, and answered my exhausted text messages through every early morning rewrite. Thank you for reminding me that courage can be quiet.

To my family and everyone who stepped in so I could step away long enough to make this book real—thank you for giving me the most valuable resource of all: time.

To Beth Collins, my lead cheerleader and unwavering voice of belief, thank you for always answering the phone and never letting me forget why this work matters. And to the rest of the Hoodrat Angels who have joined our elephant circle over the years.

To my ride-or-die colleagues, researchers, and co-conspirators—Olga Odeide, Erica Waayenberg, and Allison Roon—thank you for being in the trenches with me. You are the thinkers, question-askers, and truth-tellers who make this work come alive every single day. You've turned data into dialogue, and research into relationships. Our trauma bonds will indeed last forever—and I wouldn't have it any other way.

To SANDOW Design Group—especially Erica Holborn and AJ Paron—thank you for believing in me and supporting this leap to study what's next.

To the brilliant Surround Podcast Network production team—Hannah Viti, Rachel Senatore, and Rob Schulte—thank you for helping me realize that I've been working on the concepts behind this book since the first episode of *Design Nerds Anonymous*. You helped me harness my passion as an audio listener and taught me how to translate that curiosity into story, and story into connection as a creator. And of course, to all of our fellow *Design Nerd* listeners.

To Heloisa Nogueira, my editor and partner in clarity—thank you for diving deep with me, challenging every idea that wasn't yet clear, and never being afraid to tell me what needed to change.

To my industry mentors who became friends and fierce supporters—Janet Collins, Rex Miller, Kendra Johnson, Abby Leopold, and Moji Akinde to name a few—thank you for modeling generosity, brilliance, and courage in equal measure. You showed up with truth, not comfort—with challenge, not flattery—and my Enneagram 8 heart felt that deeply as love and respect.

To Jessica Jenkins Dalton, who not only helped conduct this research but challenged me to see its relevance far beyond our industry. You were the spark that set the ideas in motion—from the first viral article to the book in your hands. I hope that baby girl sees what a powerful force her mama can be.

To Allison Barmann, whose single recommendation set off a chain of events that led me to the TEDx stage—and to the entire TEDx Fargo team for your support, kindness, and for creating a platform where ideas like these could take root and grow. Through that journey, I also met the unbelievably talented (and patient) Deb Golden, who not only wrote the foreword to this book but became a mentor and friend for life. She's far more than an impressive title at an impressive company—she's an extraordinary human, and I'm endlessly grateful our paths crossed.

And finally, to every member of the ThinkLab community—from our Gen Z cohort to our design and manufacturer partners—thank you for your curiosity and candor. You've reminded me again and again that research is most powerful when it's a conversation, not a conclusion.

This book belongs to all of you—the ones who are rethinking what work can be and who are bold enough to build what's next.

About the Author

DESIGNER BY DEGREE. *Journalist by accident. Researcher by choice.*
With an undergraduate degree in Product Design and an MBA in Marketing, Amanda Schneider, LEED AP, MBA, is a researcher, entrepreneur, and storyteller who uses data to spark *vu-ja-de* moments—those powerful shifts where something familiar suddenly looks entirely new. Her mission? To use research not just to explain what's changing, but to help people *see differently*—so they can lead, sell, and connect more meaningfully in a world that's constantly evolving.

Amanda is the Founder + President at ThinkLab, a research and content studio at the intersection of data, design, and human behavior. She built it from the ground up—then scaled it into a thriving platform that was acquired by SANDOW, parent company of *Interior Design* magazine and one of the most influential media brands in her industry.

Her work has struck a chord on a global stage. Amanda's TEDx Fargo talk was selected by TED to be launched on TED.com—an honor granted to 1 in 18,000 TEDx talks worldwide. Her writing has appeared in viral articles in *Forbes, The Huffington Post, MIT Sloan Management Review*, and many more publications. Her podcast, *Design Nerds Anonymous*, is in the top 1% globally.

When she's not decoding behavioral shifts or translating research into aha moments, you'll find her raiding her secret stash of dark chocolate, keeping up (mostly) with her three sons (hence the *hidden* chocolate), or trail running at freakishly early hours of the morning.

Index